CLOUDBASE CHRONICLES
LIFE AT THE TOP

The CLOUDBASE CHRONICLES
LIFE AT THE TOP

Living and working at Chicago's John Hancock Center -
An engineer's tale.

HARRY W. BUDGE III

Outskirts Press, Inc.
Denver, Colorado

The opinions expressed in this manuscript are solely the opinions of the author and do not represent the opinions or thoughts of the publisher. The author has represented and warranted full ownership and/or legal right to publish all the materials in this book.

The Cloudbase Chronicles - Life at the Top
Living and working at Chicago's John Hancock Center - An engineer's tale.
All Rights Reserved.
Copyright © 2009 Harry W. Budge III
v3.0

Cover Photo © 2009 JupiterImages Corporation. All rights reserved - used with permission.

This book may not be reproduced, transmitted, or stored in whole or in part by any means, including graphic, electronic, or mechanical without the express written consent of the publisher except in the case of brief quotations embodied in critical articles and reviews.

Outskirts Press, Inc.
http://www.outskirtspress.com

ISBN: 978-1-4327-4733-6

Outskirts Press and the "OP" logo are trademarks belonging to Outskirts Press, Inc.

PRINTED IN THE UNITED STATES OF AMERICA

Contents

Contents..v
Mrs. Newton and Ulysses 1
Call Me, Kayla 29
Our Engineer Sucks!... 37
Mrs. Cosentino and the Whatcha-ma-call-it............ 47
Don't Mess with Boomer 59
9/11 73
The Alejandro Affair 107
The Great Newspaper Caper 123
Water, Weenies and Wackos................................ 141
Just another Day 161
Epilogue 175

Mrs. Newton and Ulysses

"Delaware One, come in."

Gimme a break, I thought. It was only an hour or so until quitting time. The voice coming from the radio belonged to the doorman, Alfred. Typically, when he called me, late on a Friday afternoon, it wasn't to wish me a nice weekend. I considered not answering, but only briefly.

"Go 'head," I answered.

"Harry, can you give Mrs. Newton a call?"

"Why?" I inquired. All I wanted to do was cruise until quitting time. I didn't need to get bogged down in something that could wait until Monday.

"She says her cat is stuck in the wall."

"Come back?" I wasn't sure I'd heard him correctly.

"She says her cat's in the wall," Alfred seemed to shout into the radio, as if to clarify his statement.

"10-4."

Groovy. I wasn't exactly sure what "the cat's in the wall" really meant. It was probably a code, like *the eagle has landed* or something, since there was no way a cat could literally get inside a wall around here. Whatever, something told me my weekend wouldn't be starting at the usual time. What a drag.

༄༄༄

For several years, I'd been employed as the chief engineer of a prominent residential community in Chicago, located in a 100-story skyscraper known as John Hancock Center. The building was actually designed as a mixed use facility, as most modern high-rise buildings are today. The lower half houses office and retail space, while the top half is reserved for luxury condominiums.

Although structurally *Big John* is one building, legally it is two. The commercial half is owned by a large real estate firm. The upper half is owned by several hundred individual owners which are collectively known as the Homeowners Association. All building mechanical systems and property lines are distinctly separate. The commercial owners employ a chief engineer for their own spaces. I was in charge of engineering and maintenance for the residential portion.

Here are some interesting facts about *Big John*. Construction was completed in 1969 and the building was opened for occupancy in 1970 as one property. The residential portion consisted of 705 rental apartments ranging from studios to four-bedrooms. The common areas of the residential portion on the 44th floor contain the Sky Lobby, a grocery store, a dry cleaner, a receiving room, and a swimming pool and fitness center.

John Hancock Center is more than 1100 feet in height (not counting the two 350 foot tall antennae) and requires more than forty elevators to service 100 stories, some traveling as fast as 1800 feet per minute. In high winds, window blinds actually sway and toilet bowls seem to have tides of their own.

To this day, John Hancock Center is still home to some of the world's loftiest residential units, which end at the 92nd floor (or about 1000 feet). Between floors 93 and 98 are radio and television broadcast equipment rooms, an observatory, a restaurant, and a lounge. The top two floors are reserved for HVAC and elevator equipment. The house window-washing rig is berthed in a garage on the roof.

The rental portion was converted to condominiums in 1973, which may have been the first time apartments were offered for sale in a mixed use building.

Employment as the Chief Engineer of a residential high-rise in Chicago usually requires living on the premises, the condominium provided rent free by the Association. That is actually the main reason I gave up the seniority and comfort level I enjoyed working as a power plant engineer.

After an excruciating divorce, I was left, for all intents and purposes, childless (except during visitation periods with my youngest son). Being demoralized and debt-ridden, the thought of living and working downtown, rent free, in the same building, seemed like a good idea at the time. A couple of years, I figured, and I would be back on my feet and ready to return to the industrial sector.

Little did I know that I was willingly entering a kind of indentured servitude. After about the first five years, I discovered that I had shackled myself in a pair of golden handcuffs. I had become addicted to the luxury of blowing my dough on boats, cars, vacations, and restaurants instead of rent, utilities, and parking.

I also realized that fighting rush hour traffic again had no appeal whatsoever. I'd gotten used to jumping out of bed at 7:30 AM, showering, shaving, dressing, and having my first cup o' joe and a cigarette at my desk by eight. And the elevator ride to the office took all of ten seconds!

The down side? Well, in addition to being on call twenty-four hours a day, the duties of chief engineer include operation, maintenance, and repair of all building mechanical systems (HVAC, domestic water supply, elevators, electrical distribution, pool maintenance, plumbing, etc.), as well as supervision of the mechanics and housekeeping staff and residential service requests. Responsibilities!

Being on call 24/7 wasn't that big a deal since I had a competent crew on site twenty-four hours a day. However, there were the occasional calls in the middle of night or on the weekends, usually pertaining to a ruptured water line or an elevator entrapment. When the crew could not resolve the situation on their own, they would call me.

"They don't give me a free place to live for nothing," I would remind my girlfriend, Kathy, while apologizing for leaving in the middle of dinner. Mostly, it was the bizarre calls that aggravated me. Like the one I'd just received.

As I headed back to my office to call Mrs. Newton, I briefly reviewed my mental file on Suite 5620. In my business, like many, clients tend to be classified by number -- in our operation; it was according to their suites.

Suite 5620, Pat Newton.

Sixty-ish, tall, frail, dark hair with touches of gray, somewhat eccentric, and most significantly to me, the owner of a devilish Persian cat named Ulysses. All in all, Mrs. Newton was all right, but I really despised that cat.

Normally, I would have radioed a mechanic or, at the least, a janitor to handle it. But, it was nearing the end of the shift and Mrs. Newton was one of those that insisted on "going to the top" for everything. Besides, I was somewhat intrigued.

I was about to hang up after 13 rings on the house phone when she answered. "Hellooo."

"Hi, Mrs. Newton, it's Harry. Alfred told me that you needed to speak to me?"

"Oh yes, thank you so much for calling," she said. "I've been just frantic."

"What seems to be the problem?" I asked with as much concern as I could muster.

"Well, Ulysses has been a naughty boy again."

Oh, now there's a surprise, I thought.

"So what's he gotten himself into this time?" The last time, it was a quart of red oil paint, which required a gallon of paint thinner, plenty of elbow grease, and half an hour of hand to talon combat to resolve.

"I know it sounds odd, but he's gotten into the wall somehow and now he can't get out."

"Are you sure he's in the wall?" I asked. I seriously doubted even Ulysses could pull that one off. After all, this was a building constructed of concrete, steel, drywall, and glass. For the sake of fire containment, there should have been no penetrations large enough for even a mouse to pass, much less a fat cat like him.

"He's in there, Harry. Please come up and see for yourself. I'm afraid he'll die in there if you don't do something!" She was starting to get really wound up.

"Not to worry, I'll be right there," I said as I hung up the phone and shook my head.

"Harry? Is that you?" asked the voice from the other side of the door.

"Yes, ma'am," I replied as I waited for the two deadbolts and several safety chains to disengage.

When she opened the door, she grabbed my right arm with both hands and proclaimed, "Thank God, you're finally here."

Of course I realized that in some situations, minutes can seem like hours, so I didn't bother mentioning that it had been less than a minute since I had spoken to her.

"So where exactly do you think he is?" I asked.

"Well I'm not sure, but I can hear him meowing over here," she said as she dragged me to the living room. "He sounds pitiful, simply pitiful. Just listen."

I couldn't hear a thing. So I told her, "I can't hear a thing."

"Well, he isn't talking now, is he?" she snapped.

"I guess not." Okay. So now I have to find a cat that is supposedly in the wall, but he isn't talking.

"Do you hear anything, Mrs. Newton?" I had to ask.

"Of course I don't. Just like everything else around here, the noise stops when the serviceman finally shows up!"

"Well, maybe I should come back when he *is* talking." I could see that the situation was going nowhere and I just wanted to get out. "You know. I need to get going now and …"

"Harry Budge. This is a matter of life or death. What could possibly be more important than saving a poor, dumb animal?"

"Well, since you put it that way…"

"Shhh! Can you hear him now?" She was really excited, but I still couldn't hear anything.

"I'm not sure, Mrs. Newton. It kinda sounded like the wind to me."

"Nonsense," she said. "I heard him plain as day. He's right in there!" She pointed toward the corner of the living room, near the window. At the ceiling in this particular corner, an "X" beam joined with the vertical column and the horizontal beams which make up the building's superstructure.

I suppose at this point it would be appropriate to describe the basic interior construction of the building.

Mrs. Newton happened to live in a unit where one of the "X" beams (second to the building's taper, the most prominent feature of the Hancock's exterior architecture) crossed the living room window bay. These "X" beams are known as "diagonals" when viewed from the inside.

Naturally, all steel support columns and beams are covered in drywall. That includes the diagonals. Therefore, nearly every room of every condo has soffits at the ceiling against the interior and exterior walls as well as vertical drywall clad columns between the window bays and rooms. And of course some units (the lucky few, in my opinion) are graced with diagonals.

Diagonals are either loved or loathed. Some folks say they block the view, while others admire the unique plane they form in their homes. The diagonal which passed through my own living room doubled as a back rest when I'd sit on the window box looking out over the city. These "window boxes," run the entire length of the window bays. A small portion of the space beneath the window boxes in each room contains an air conditioning unit -- the rest of the space is empty.

Anyway, back to the matter at hand.

I walked over to the corner she indicated and strained my ears. Still, I heard nothing. I was about to say as much when from behind me began the most hideous screech I had ever heard. I'm not kidding.

"Ulyyyysses! Ulyyyysses, you beautiful boyyyoyy!" Evidently, Mrs. Newton fancied herself an opera singer in years gone by.

"Ulyyyysses, come to Maaaamaaa!"

I'd have given anything for a pair of ear plugs right about then.

"He loves to sing with me, you know," she told me between wails. I was about to beg her to let me go when I heard a muffled meow.

"See! I told you! Did you hear that?" she asked.

"Yes Ma'am, I heard it. But I couldn't quite make out exactly where it came from."

"I'm telling you, he's right in there, inside the wall," she said with authority.

I must have looked somewhat skeptical, so she said, "Watch, I'll show you," and began howling again. "Ulyyyysses!" And I'll be damned if the cat didn't start wailing back!

⁂

Initially, it sounded to me like the meows were coming from the soffit. As I pondered the situation, I surveyed the room for possible access points to the walls' interior. There were no obvious holes anywhere. However, as my gaze panned past the window, I noticed that the grate which normally covers the discharge of the air conditioning unit in the window box was lying on the floor.

"Mrs. Newton. Why is the A/C grate on the floor?" I asked.

"Oh, I dropped a pen in there last night, so I had to take the grate off to get it out."

As I walked over to the window I started congratulating myself, convinced that I had this deal all worked out, yet marveling at how the cat had learned to project his voice.

Simple, I thought. Reach inside, grab the cat, drag him out, maybe get a tip and I'm out the door. So I pulled out the little penlight I always carried and peered down through the grate opening into the void between the A/C unit and the diagonal. Unfortunately, instead of finding a mangy Persian cat, what I found was an 8" x 8" opening in the drywall cladding of the diagonal. Damn! This was really going to suck.

"Well, Mrs. Newton, looks like I found the problem," I said over my shoulder.

"You mean you can see Ulysses?" she asked hopefully.

"No. I mean I can see a hole under the window box where he was able to get into the wall."

"Well, can't you just reach down in there and get him out?" she asked.

"No ma'am. I can't even see him."

"Ulyyyysses! Who's the most beauty-full boy in the wor-hurld," she shrieked, without warning, into my ear.

Please God, make her stop, I silently pleaded. *It's Friday night, I have my son for the weekend and I need to hit the road to pick him up before the Kennedy becomes a parking lot. Please make this stupid cat come out so I can leave.*

"Ulyyysses! Come out for mommy!"

Okay. Just… chill. We can work this out.

"Mrs. Newton, it looks like we're going to have to cut a hole in the wall to get him out, okay?"

"I don't care what it takes, Harry. Just get him out of there!" she demanded.

"All right, Mrs. Newton, I'll have to go and get some tools. I'll be back in just a few minutes," I promised as I headed out the door. As I did, I heard the kitty serenade beginning once again.

Down in the shop, I took a five minute smoke break and collected up the tools I thought I would need to free Ulysses.

Let's see, tarp, hand tools, HEPA vacuum, goggles, and most important, the Sawzall. Yeah. The trusty Sawzall would make short work of the drywall standing between me and my freedom, or Ulysses' freedom, depending on how one looked at it.

"Mrs. Newton, I'm back," I called out as I walked into the apartment. I had thrown the deadbolt while the door was open when I left. This allowed me to walk right in and save precious minutes when I returned. After all, it was Friday night and I wanted to get going. Rush hour on the Kennedy was building and Li'l Harry and I had plans. And, well…you get the picture.

"It's about time. Did you decide to take a break while Ulysses is dying in the wall?" she asked, sarcastically.

"Uh, no ma'am. It just took a while to get an elevator," I lied.

"Well, if you say so. Please just rescue Ulysses now."

"Yes ma'am, but you might want to go and have a cup of tea in the kitchen. It's going to get awfully noisy and dusty in here."

"Not so fast," she said. "Where are you going to cut this hole?"

"Well, I thought I'd cut right up here in the soffit since this is where it sounds like he is," I said, pointing to a spot near the ceiling at the front (window) end of the apartment.

"Why that's ridiculous!" she said. "How could he possibly get up in there?"

Yeah, I see what you mean. Getting into the wall in the first place is completely understandable, but getting into the wall and then up into the soffit, well that's just crazy talk.

"All right, ma'am, where do **you** think I should start?" I asked. I was starting to cop a 'tude.

"How about. . . right there?" she said as she pointed to a spot near the floor on a common interior wall.

"Mrs. Newton. There's only about an inch and a half of space in that wall. Besides, there's a stud every sixteen inches. There's no way he could have gotten inside."

"Well, he sounds like he's in there to me, so just cut the hole and look," she insisted.

"Ma'am, if I cut a hole there, you will have a pass through to your master bedroom," I explained.

"I don't care what you say, Harry. I think he's in there. So I want you to cut a hole, right there, right now, and that's final."

All right, I give up. "Yes ma'am. But I still say you should leave the room; it's going to get noisy and really dusty."

"Fine. Call me when you have him out." And she headed to the kitchen.

Time for Dr. Sawzall.

For those unfamiliar with power tools, a Sawzall is a reciprocating electric/battery powered saw which is considered to be an essential tool to building operations and maintenance. The frequency of leaks, unexplained noise, etc. requires quick access to ceilings and walls. And when it comes to cutting holes, Dr. Sawzall is second to none. Let me put it this way: locksmiths have picks, engineers have the Dr.

After laying down some tarps below the designated area, I unleashed my little friend with the eight-inch teeth. Within a minute I had about a two by two-foot square window cut from the living room to the master bedroom. Just like I said, "Ain't no cats in this wall."

"Mrs. Newton, could you come here, please?" I calmly called, with more than a little satisfaction in my voice.

"Did you get him out?" she asked as she walked into the room.

"No -- as I explained, there's no room in this wall for him to squeeze into. See?" I stated as I directed her vision to the new penetration.

As she was looking through the hole into her bedroom, I noticed her head cocked to the side, as if listening, but not in the direction of where I wanted to cut. Then she started looking at the vertical column near the bedroom window.

"I think you should let me..."

"Over there. He's in there." Now she was pointing through the hole. "Quick, cut a hole over there before he moves again."

Oh god, here we go again. "Mrs. Newton, I really think he's over here, up in the soffit."

"No, he's in there, I'm sure of it," she said. "Come now. Ulysses is waiting." And she headed off to the master bedroom.

Two holes later, still no Ulysses, and I'm about to flip out on the old bag. She won't even consider that I might be right as to the location of her precious little peckerhead. She's getting more flustered by the minute and I'm running late for my trek up the Kennedy to get my son for the weekend. Late? Hell, too late is more like it. It'll take at least an hour to go fifteen miles now. Just one more reason to hate that cat.

"Mrs. Newton, look, I have to go get my son out on the northwest side. Maybe now, with these holes opened up, Ulysses will come out on his own if we just leave him be." It seemed reasonable to me. For all I knew, the little bastard really was toying with me; moving from place to place, just to piss me off.

"No, we need to rescue him. He hasn't had any food or water for more than two hours."

Oh shit, two whole hours. He'll surely die if he doesn't pig out, like...soon!

"Okay," I said. "How about this then? Let's put some food and water by each of the holes. I'll go and get little Harry. While I'm gone, you can sing to him and whatnot, and try to coax him out. I'll check with you when I get back. If he's not out by the time I get back, then we'll come up with another plan." I knew that fat cat wouldn't forgo stuffing his face for very long.

"But how long will you be gone?" she asked in a distressed voice while twisting her hankie into knots.

"Oh, I should think at this time of day, about two hours round trip (for all of thirty miles.) I'll be back about eight, all right?"

"Well...all right. But promise me you'll stop back as soon as you return.

"Of course I will," I assured her. "I won't let anything bad happen to Ulysses. We'll get him out, I promise." One way or another, I thought.

)))(

The trip out on the Kennedy went about as I expected. Bumper-to-bumper the whole way out and the whole way back.

Harry was wired up about what we were going to do over the weekend. He was all "Can we go to the park?" and "can we go to the kids' museum at Navy Pier?" Then it was about thirty minutes of "Poke'mon this" and "Poke'mon that." "Blah, blah, blah." Anyway, between the jabber and the traffic, by the time we got back to the building, my head was splitting.

"Now Harry, before we do anything I have to stop at this lady's house."

"How come, Dad?"

"Well, because her cat got himself stuck in the wall and we have to rescue him."

"Okay. But Dad, can I ask you something?"

"Sure, Harry. What is it?"

"How did the cat get in the wall?" I knew he was going to ask me that. "I never heard of a cat getting stuck in a wall before. I thought cats got stuck in trees."

"Yes Harry, that's usually true. But this cat never goes outside so he's probably never even seen a tree."

"So he gets stuck in walls instead?" he asked with a doubtful look on his face.

"Yes, Harry, something like that."

"But, Dad, can I ask you something else?"

(Sigh) "Yes, Harry." Here it comes, I thought. The mother of all his maddening questions. "What's on your mind?"

With a serious tone in his voice, and a puzzled look on his face, he asked, "Aren't firemen supposed to be in charge of saving cats?"

⁂

After about twenty minutes of explaining to my son why I was in charge of this particular cat rescue, we were at the door of 5620.

"Now Harry, you behave yourself. And be polite to Mrs. Newton. If we're lucky the cat's already come out by himself and we can go home and play *Sorry!* or something, okay?"

"Okay, Dad."

As I knocked on the door, we could hear Mrs. Newton serenading Ulysses.

"Ulyyysses. Come out for Maaamaa. Come and get your Friskies!"

"Is the lady singing, Dad?"

"Yes, Harry, if you can call it that." I knocked again.

"How come?"

"Because she thinks the cat will come out of the wall if she sings to him." Once again, I knocked.

"Why?"

"I don't know, Harry. Just because. Enough with the questions for now, all right?"

"Okay, Dad."

I just couldn't take any more questions, so I started banging on the door with both hands as hard as I could. Finally the singing stopped and I could hear her walking toward the door.

"Harry is that you?" she asked without opening the door.

"Yes, Mrs. Newton. It's me and my son, Harry."

"Geez, the way you were banging on the door, you nearly scared the life out of me," she said as the bolts and chains were sliding back. "I thought it was some kind of rapist or a robber or something."

"Yeah, whatever," I muttered under my breath as the door opened.

"What was that?" she snapped.

"Are things any *better*?" I asked, with the emphasis on better.

"He's not out of the wall yet, if that's what you mean," she said as she gave me the evil eye.

"Well, I'll get back to it and I expect I'll have him safe and sound in no time. Oh, by the way, Mrs. Newton, this is Harry the Fourth." Yeah, yeah, I know. What can I say? I didn't want to break the chain.

Now, Mrs. Newton may have been cranky, but when she saw Harry her eyes simply lit up. Turns out she loved children and had an extremely high tolerance for meaningless chatter. This was positively a match made in heaven. Harry loved to blab and she loved to listen. As she led Harry away to the kitchen for some milk and cookies I wondered how much time I had before they both got bored and came back to torment me.

I had decided to use scientific deduction and geometric logic (like Bogart in *The Caine Mutiny*) to determine the precise location of Mr. Ulysses before I made my next exploratory hole. In other words, I was going to think about it for a few minutes before I started hacking into the walls again. After all, if I cut the cat in half, locating and retrieving him would not have mattered much. You can see the dilemma.

Up until then, I knew that there was no way of injuring the cat. That was because I was sure he was nowhere near where Mrs. Newton was insisting I cut. But now, if I started chopping near where I believed him to be, I risked injuring him (or worse) in the process. The image of a magician, bisecting his lovely assistant while she lay in the magic box with head and feet protruding from either end, flashed across my mind. I'd always wondered what the result would look like if the magic didn't work.

Anyway, after about ten minutes of concentrated deliberation, I was about to proceed when...

"What are you waiting for, Harry? I'd have thought you'd have him out by now." She was back.

"Whatcha doin', Dad?" Harry, the indefatigable question machine, was back as well.

"Well, I was just about to cut a hole up here in the soffit. But, you're both going to have to leave. All the dust and noise isn't good for you."

Truthfully, I didn't particularly care for anyone watching me work. It made me nervous. But I wasn't kidding about the dust and the racket. It wasn't good for anyone. This is why I always wore ear plugs, goggles, and a dust mask when making that kind of mess.

"That's fine, Harry. But I think you should cut over there." Here she goes again, I silently lamented.

"Mrs. Newton, that wall separates this room from the closet on the other side. If I cut there, you'll wind up with another window like the one over there," I pointed.

"I think you should cut there anyway."

Okay, now I'm pissed. Fine. No more Mr. Nice Guy. You want some holes, lady? I'll give you some holes. When I'm done, this place is gonna look like a hunk of Swiss cheese!

"All right, Mrs. Newton, if you insist. I'll cut wherever you say. But I need you to take Harry out of the room. I'll call you after I cut the hole."

And so it went. I'd cut holes wherever she said. Then I'd call her back from the kitchen. Of course she'd bring Harry with her to assist in antagonizing me. Then she'd tell me where to cut next. Predictably, Ulysses was nowhere to be found. The whole time, she was getting more and more agitated, I was getting more and more frustrated and Harry was getting more and more confused.

"Dad, why do you keep cutting holes in different places?"

"Because I'm trying to find the cat."

"Why don't you cut the hole where the cat is?"

"Because..." before I stuck my foot squarely in my mouth, out of the corner of my eye I noticed Mrs. Newton standing there with arms folded, obviously eavesdropping. "Well, because I don't know exactly where he is."

"How come he won't come out, Dad?"

"Because he's a dumb animal, Harry." was all I could say.

Of course, about every five minutes or so, Mrs. Newton started her wailing. She didn't stop until Doofus answered so we could all be sure he wasn't dead.

Along about ten o'clock I said to Mrs. Newton, "I think we should call it a night now, Mrs. Newton. I'm sure he'll come out when he's thirsty enough or hungry enough." She looked like she was going to have a stroke.

"Please, Harry. You can't give up. He'll die in there!" Her voice was sort of quivering and I knew it was only seconds before the dam broke.

"I'm not giving up, Mrs. Newton. I say we just give it a break for tonight. If he doesn't come out by morning I'll come back and tear out the walls completely if I have to. I swear I won't let Ulysses die."

"Well, all right then. What time will you come back?" she asked as she began tying her handkerchief into a bunch again.

"How 'bout I call you first thing in the morning, say eight o'clock, all right?"

"Okay, if you think that's best."

"I honestly do, Mrs. Newton. All this noise and excitement probably has him all freaked out. It will do him good to have some peace and quiet for awhile."

And so, Harry and I went home to get some of our own peace and quiet.

◗◗◗◖

I'm on a roll. I've won, like, at least a grand at the roulette table. Now I'm at the craps table, cleaning house. I've got a fat cigar in one hand and a martini in the other. The kid rolling the dice just won't crap out. Man, this is great! The place is going wild. Sounds like somebody just won big on a slot machine. The alarm is screaming for an attendant. Hey, it's Kathy. She just won the progressive jackpot on the Wheel of Fortune machine. I grab my chips and start heading over toward my baby when someone starts shoving me. Hey. Lay off, man. Now, the alarm is getting louder and the shoving is getting harder and...

"Dad, wake up." Harry was shaking me. "The telephone keeps ringing in the living room."

"Huh? What?"

"Dad, wake up. The telephone in the living room won't stop ringing and I'm scared to pick it up." Harry was only five at the time and he didn't like to answer the phone. The fog started to clear.

"What did you say, Hairball?"

"The telephone in the living room is ringing. You know, the one on the wall."

Now I got it. The siren in my dream was actually the house phone, which meant we weren't rich. This also meant that either one of the crew or one of the doormen was trying to reach me. They had gotten accustomed to letting the house phone ring a long time, since it was near the entry door, which was some distance from the master bedroom.

Groggily, I made my way to the living room, picked up the phone and said, "Hello?"

"Harry. This is Alfred. Mrs. Newton called and said it was an emergency and that you need to call her right away."

Crap! "What time is it, Al?"

"Right now it's 8:02 AM., Harry."

"Thanks, Alfred."

This could only mean one thing. I wasn't gonna be lying around reading the paper and drinking coffee all morning.

I dialed Mrs. Newton's unit on the house phone, which I should explain is strictly for internal communications, as in a hotel. In this case, I could call any condo or common area with a four-digit number, but residents were blocked from calling me. I wasn't going for that old *Honeymooners* crap. No way. Remember the episode where Ralph took the job of the building super and installed a buzzer system? Norton kept calling him every five minutes to come up and plunge the toilet or change a light bulb or something. Around here, if anyone wanted to get in touch with me, they had to go through the doorman first.

"Is that you, Harry?" asked a high-pitched voice at the other end of the line. This wasn't good. She sounded kinda hysterical.

"Yes, Mrs. Newton. It's me. Is everything all right?"

"Nooooo. Everything is not all right. You have to get down here right away and rescue poor Ulysses before he dies. He's been trapped in there all night and now he won't talk to me, even when I sing."

Imagine that. And her, with such an angelic voice.

"I'll be down in about half an hour, then."

"No, you need to come right now. I won't stand for my Ulysses being entrapped another minute. Not another minute. Do you hear me?" She droned on and on like that while I held the phone away from my ear.

"Mrs. Newton," I finally interrupted, with as much courtesy as I could muster under the circumstances. "I said I will be down in half an hour. I need to have some coffee, wake up and feed my son. Then I'll be down."

"Harry Budge! I said this couldn't wait and I meant it. Now I don't care about any of your excuses, I demand that you get here now!"

Right! That was the way wrong thing to say to me at eight in the morning. Especially after waking me up in the middle of an awesome dream and wasting my time on a Friday night. Before I even had my first cup of coffee! I blew a gasket.

"Let me tell you something, Mrs. Newton. I am the chief engineer. Not the animal control warden. My contract does not require me to demolish condominium interiors for any reason. And it certainly doesn't require me to spend my off hours searching for a cat that is too stupid to find his way out of a place he got himself into. And, furthermore..."

Before I got to finish my dissertation, she was sobbing into the phone.

"You're a horrible, evil man. You're just going to let a poor defenseless animal perish in the wall. (Sob) What a big man you are. (Sniff) Blah, blah, blah...(sob)...I hope you're satisfied when Ulysses is dead and gone and..."

I gently hung up the phone and took a deep breath.

"Harry, get dressed."

"Why, Dad?"

"Cuz we're going on a guilt trip."

"Whatcha mean, Dad? What about my cartoons?"

"Just get dressed, Harry. We have to go down to Mrs. Newton's house again and try to save Ulysses."

Knock, knock, knock.

No answer.

I knocked again. "Mrs. Newton," I shouted through the locked door. "It's Harry and Harry. We've come to get Ulysses out of the wall."

Through the door: (Sniffle) "You don't care if he dies alone in the wall. (Sob) To you he's just a fat dumb cat. You don't care if he's the only friend I have left in the world. Ooooohhh, hooooooooo, hooooooo."

Okay, I'll admit it. She was getting to me.

"Please, Mrs. Newton. Open the door. I'm sorry. I didn't mean to shout at you. You know I don't want anything bad to happen to Ulysses. C'mon, now."

"I called Mrs. Stevens from down the hall. (Sob) She's going to come and help me."

Yeah, right. Mrs. Stevens, the other psycho cat lady. She was about ninety and needed a walker to get around. That's what I called the blind leading the blind. But this was the medicine I deserved for losing my temper and I had to take it.

"Please, Mrs. Newton. I'm sorry. Now let me in so I can get to work. Besides, little Harry is here and he's worried about Ulysses too."

Worked like a charm. I knew she'd fall for the old "worried little kid" trick. I heard the bolts and chains sliding and jingling and soon the door was open. Her eyes were puffy and she looked like she'd been up all night worrying.

"I haven't slept a wink. Please, Harry. Get him out of there before he dies."

She was about to turn on the water works again so I put my arm around her shoulder and said, "I'm sorry, Mrs. Newton. Let's start over." Harry was just standing there, looking kinda lost, so I said, "Hey, Hairball. Why don't you go to the kitchen with Mrs. Newton and help her make some coffee? Maybe you can tell her about Poke'mon or something."

"Okay, Dad." Harry came over and took Mrs. Newton's hand and started leading her to the kitchen.

Just then a knock came at the door. "I'll get it, Mrs. Newton." I walked over to the entry door and opened it to find Mrs. Stevens, who resembled Mrs. Butterworth on steroids, standing there with her three wheeled walker, scowling at me as if I was something a person wouldn't want to step in.

"Humph," was the only sound she made as she ran over my foot and bulldozed her way through the door.

"Hello, Pat. Are you all right, dear? I see Mr. Big Shot finally decided to show up. I hope he came to do something besides wreck your walls today."

With that she noticed Harry and said, "Oh. And who might this handsome young man be?"

"This is Harry's son who is also named Harry. He seems to be a very nice young man," Mrs. Newton informed her.

That's when they both turned to look at me with that disdainful old lady look one more time before they stuck their noses in the air and headed off to the kitchen with Harry in tow. As they walked away, I could hear one of them say something about him probably taking after his mother.

Alrighty, then. Now it was time to put this little caper to bed. I surveyed the battlefield. Some collateral damage. Seven sizable holes. No big deal for Bill, the house painter. He'd make short work of that mess. Of course it would be Alan the property manager's job to sort out the repair charges. Not my deal. My problem was getting the stupid cat out of the stupid wall in one stupid piece.

So. Hmmm. Where to start? If I was smart, all it would take was one properly located hole and I could grab the cat, pass him off to his mommy, and split. I looked up at the soffit and followed it to the corner where it connected to the one above the window as well as the diagonal which intersected the window wall. Just about a foot from the corner; that was the bull's eye.

I donned my goggles and respirator and stepped up on the ladder. I knocked on the soffit more out of habit than anything else. Then I picked up the Sawzall and fired it up. Eighteen volts of pure, reciprocating, cutting power. Slowly, with the precision of a surgeon, I made the first incision. I ran the hungry blade horizontally, from left to right. After about six inches, I hit a metal stud. Agggh! Freak out! Don't forget what's on the other side, dumbass. Whew! It's cool. I recovered my composure and carried on for another foot. When I reached the end of my cut, I withdrew the blade and held it up for inspection. So far, so good. No blood, no fur. And no sickening feline cries. That was good. That was real good.

Next, I repeated the maneuver about twelve inches above the first, an inch or so from the ceiling. Still, there were no signs of organic residue on the blade.

I was in the zone now. It was time now for the vertical cuts which would connect the previous ones to form a square shaped doorway to freedom — for both Ulysses and me. First the left side, top to bottom. No problem. Finally, I cut the right side. Everything was cool. I extracted the blade to reveal nothing more insidious than some telltale asbestos fibers. Not something you would want to be breathing on a regular basis, but safe enough where it was for the time being.

Now, for the moment of truth. I inserted the blade of my knife into the bottom slit and pried out the square of dry wall to expose... an asbestos-coated steel "I" beam. No cat. But wait, I heard a rustling noise coming from the hole.

"Here, kitty. Here, kitty." Yeah well, I knew it wouldn't be that easy. Climbing up one more step I peered into the hole. Looking to the right, toward the corner, the first thing I noticed was lots of asbestos. As my eyes began adjusting to the darkness, I saw two luminescent orbs reflecting back at me. Yeah, baby! It's Ulysses.

"Here, kitty." Nope. He wasn't coming out. So I got my maglight out to get a better look. I peered in the direction of the eyes and here's what I saw:

A big, fat, ginger colored cat, dusted from head to foot with asbestos fibers. The flashlight revealed that he had gotten where he was by climbing up the diagonal beam (also covered with asbestos) and was perched on the horizontal beam. There was no apparent reason why he couldn't have exited the way he came. To me, it looked like he just didn't want to come out. In fact, with my flashlight off, I could actually see daylight shining up from the hole at the bottom of the diagonal where he had entered in the first place. I tried coaxing and cursing for several minutes, but he wasn't going for any of it. Other options crossed my mind, none of which would have been endorsed by PETA.

There was obviously only one way to get that dumbass out of the wall. By force!

So I reached into the hole with my left arm and grabbed the collar around Ulysses' neck. And what a fine handle it made. Unfortunately, Ulysses wasn't ready to leave his nest just then. So as I started to pull, he started to hiss. Then he dug his paws into the insulation and started to back up. That's when the collar slipped over his head. Damn!

I wasn't about to lose my prize, so I reached as far as I could, grabbed him by the scruff of his neck and dragged him through the asbestos for about two feet until I could get my other hand on him and yank him from the hole.

Well, rather than shred me to pieces as I expected, Old Fatso settled down immediately, which was a good thing, because with all the asbestos in his fur, he could have qualified as his own EPA haz-mat event.

I strode off to the kitchen to present Ulysses to Mrs. Newton. The second I walked through the doorway, she screamed and ran over to rip the cat from my arms. Before I could caution her about the asbestos, she had her face buried in his fur and was slobbering all over him.

"Oh, my poor Ulysses! You beautiful boy. Mommy was so worried about you. I'm sorry it took so long for Harry to rescue you."

I didn't have the heart to tell her that he was, at that point, carcinogenic.

Now, I know it was just my imagination, but at the time I would have sworn that the cat was giving me a look, as if to say, "Na, Na, Na, Na, Na. I'm the king of the world!"

I figured my work was done so I called the crew on my radio to come to the condo to grab the tools, clean up the debris and temporarily seal the holes until Monday morning. Then Bill would perform the necessary drywall repairs. It was all over now but the accolades and the reward. After all, I was a hero, right?

"Well, it's time to go now, Harry." I thought that once we started heading for the door, Mrs. Newton would start thanking me and whipping out the Jacksons.

As Harry got up to leave the kitchen table, Mrs. Newton gave him ten bucks and said, loudly enough for me to get the message, "Now that's your money, sweetheart -- and you buy whatever you want."

"Isn't he a delightful little boy?" she asked Mrs. Stevens, who smiled and nodded her head in agreement.

Then she turned to me. Finally! This part made all the aggravation worthwhile. Based on what she gave Harry just for blabbing, my tip ought to be pretty sweet.

"Now, Harry, you are going to ensure that all these holes are repaired, including the one where Ulysses got in, correct?"

"Um, yes ma'am," I said. But meanwhile, I was thinking, hey, what's the deal? Where's the gratitude; the tearful thanks? Where's the purse?!

"I'll expect Bill here bright and early Monday morning. Now I suppose I need to give Ulysses a bath. His fur is absolutely dreadful."

Then she turned and walked off toward the master bathroom with the little weasel/cat looking back at me, over her shoulder. However, just then there came a knock at the door so she turned back to answer it.

"Who is it?"

"Maintenance, ma'am."

When she opened the door, two janitors, Pete and Clemente, were there, as was the shift mechanic, Carlos, who stepped up and said, "We're here to clean up and put things back in order ma'am."

"Yes, yes. Thank you so much for coming. Come right on in boys. I can't tell you how much I appreciate all your help."

Then she marched off with Ulysses toward the bathroom.

Talk about a bloody nose! I stood there for a second, being invisible. Carlos walked over to me, just to see if there were any specific orders.

"Just cover the holes, clean up the dust and do whatever else she wants." Then, in a lowered voice, "I do <u>not</u> want to be called back to this apartment for any reason. Got it?"

He nodded and proceeded to the living room to get started with the other guys.

By this time, Mrs. Stevens was standing with her walker in the hallway outside the bathroom and I could hear water running. For all intents and purposes, I had been dismissed.

It was time to go. I looked down at Harry who until then had been quietly admiring his ten dollar bill.

"So, what are you gonna buy with your ten dollars, Harry?" I asked as we left the apartment.

"Well, I was kinda saving up for something."

"Oh, yeah? What, a skateboard or a video game or something?"

"No, Dad, nothing like that."

"Well? What then?"

With innocent eyes and smile on his face, he looked up and asked, "Dad, how much do kittens cost?"

Call Me, Kayla

Kayla was a working girl. Not the North Avenue streetwalking kind. More like the escort service kind. She was apparently a former *Miss Something or Other* sometime during her teens, and had somehow parlayed that distinction into a minor modeling career. She was kinda cute when she was young, in a sultry, olive skinned, Mediterranean sort of way. That was when she was in her twenties. (She had photos of herself in her glory days plastered all over her apartment). But in her late thirties, it seemed her work consisted more of entertaining rich old business men, in town and out. An endless procession of male "associates" would call on her at all hours when she was in town.

On any given day, a flower delivery could be found outside her door. Unfortunately for the staff, the attention did nothing for her disposition. Most times, she was aloof and condescending. Sometimes she was downright rude. To say the least, she wasn't very popular with the crew. The maintenance guys would shuffle her service requests back and forth until I was forced to assign them specifically to somebody. I guess it's true; beauty really is only skin deep.

❧❧❧

When the house phone rang I was watching my second episode of Star Trek (Monday was *Star Trek* night on the Sci-Fi channel).

Spock was doing a mind meld on a rock creature that had been killing some miners. I had just poured a glass of port and microwaved a bag of popcorn. Needless to say, I did not want to be disturbed.

"Chief? It's Jim. Sorry to bother you, but we have a situation at 6211."

6211 was Kayla's place, and any "situation" which involved Kayla was bound to be a pain in the ass.

"Yeah, what's the problem?"

"Well, she called us complaining that one of the smoke detectors in her apartment was chirping and it was driving her nuts. So Dave and I went up there to check it out. We heard the sound that she was griping about, but we didn't think it was coming from a smoke. Anyway, after her ragging us about not knowing our jobs and such we pulled the batteries out of every smoke head in the place and the sound is still there."

"Well it's obviously not a smoke detector then, is it?" I said, as I craned my neck to see what Captain Kirk was doing.

"Yeah, we know that, but she demanded that we get you down there. She was really getting snotty so we told her we would contact you, and left to come down to the office to call."

Okay, now Bones was doing surgery on the rock creature because the miners had shot it with a phaser before Spock had performed his mind reading trick. Of course, the creature would survive and it and the miners would make up and be friends because it was all a big misunderstanding. I knew that because, well...every *Trekkie* knows that story. But damn it, I wanted to chill and watch it again.

"Chief? You coming?" Jim asked.

"What?" I asked as Bones finished the concrete bandage on the rock.

"Are you coming? She's pretty pissed."

I was beginning to get pissed myself. I realized that I was going to have to take care of this or they'd be calling every five minutes. Or worse, she'd get my home number from 411 and then call me on my land line herself. That would really set me off and then I would lose it and say something I'd regret and, well, it wouldn't be good.

"Yeah, yeah, yeah. You guys head back to her place and I'll meet you there."

I guess what was really bugging me was this chick's attitude. We weren't a rental building and it really wasn't our problem if she had some unexplained beeping sound coming from somewhere in her apartment. As long as it wasn't a building system, like the smoke detectors which we had already ruled out, then we were under no obligation to waste time at her place. Particularly since it was practically guaranteed that she would refuse to pay for the time we spent looking for the phantom noise.

Keep in mind; this was a woman that went by only one name. You know, like *Fabio* or *God*. I've learned over the years that anyone that self-important is never a pleasure to deal with.

꩜꩜꩜

On the way down to 6211, I considered possible sources of the mysterious noise. Smoke detectors were out. Maybe the dishwasher or the stove? Modern appliances sometimes made sounds to alert the home owner that a door was ajar, etc. I only hoped that it was something simple so I could get back to the crew of *Starship Enterprise* before the start of the next episode.

Knock, knock.

Jim opened the door. As I entered I saw *The Kayla* standing there in the dining area with her arms crossed and her right hip out in an obvious display of contempt.

"So, what seems to be the problem here this evening?" I asked her as I walked into the room.

"The problem," she snarled, "is that these incompetent fools can't seem to locate the noise that's been driving me crazy for the past four hours. I told them it's a smoke detector but they won't listen."

I turned to Jim, who just shrugged. Dave, meanwhile, was busy inspecting the toes of his shoes over by the door.

"It doesn't do it continually. It comes and goes every few minutes. Ask 'em. They heard it."

As I turned to speak to Jim, he said, "That's right, Chief.. We heard it but it wasn't coming from a smoke detector. It didn't even sound like a smoke detector."

"I'm telling you it's a goddamn smoke detector," spat Kayla.

"Okay, what exactly did it sound like?" I asked without directing the question to anyone in particular.

"Like a smoke detector," she averred.

"Not like a smoke detector. More like, uh, uh, I don't know, a different kind of beeping sound," said Jim.

"I think it sounded more like a robot," Dave chimed in.

"Huh?" the rest of us said in unison as we all looked at him incredulously.

"Well, it sounds like the one my kid has at home," Dave clarified, kind of bashfully as he resumed his shoe inspection.

"Well it isn't a stupid...Wait! There it is! Shut up and listen," Kayla shouted.

Sure enough, there it was. A faint, beep...beep...beep. Beep...beep...beep. Beep...beep...beep. Then it quit.

"See, I told you it's a smoke detector."

"No, ma'am, that's not the sound a smoke detector makes," I replied. "Anyway, the batteries have already been removed from all the smoke detectors. But, just to be sure, we'll remove all the smoke detectors from the apartment, okay?"

"Well, if it's not a smoke detector, then just what the hell is it?" she asked with obvious disdain.

"I don't know, but I'll do my best to find out." Then, to Jim, "Remove all the smokes and take them out to the corridor."

"10-4, Chief."

"Now," I said, as I turned to Kayla, "let's check out the kitchen. Maybe an appliance is in trouble."

"Yeah, right, dumbass," I heard her mumble, under her breath.

I ignored the insult as I headed toward the kitchen and said, "Sometimes, appliances give warning sounds to let you know, say, that the microwave is finished cooking, or the freezer door is ajar."

"Listen. I didn't just move in yesterday. I've lived here for fifteen years. I think I would know the sounds my appliances make by now," she hissed. "The only beeping sound I've ever heard came from a smoke detector when there was something wrong with it." She was sounding arrogant now and really getting on my nerves.

"Well, let's just give it a minute to..." There it was again. Beep... beep...beep. Beep...beep...beep. Beep...beep...beep. Then it was gone.

"Guess we can definitively rule out smoke detectors now, once and for all," I said with satisfaction. "In fact, now I'm sure that it's coming from somewhere here in this kitchen."

The sound was definitely close so I began a systematic inspection of every appliance. Microwave. . . nothing. Dishwasher....same thing. Range. . . nada. Hell, I even checked the toaster oven. Nothing indicated a problem. So then I said to Jim, "Turn off all the appliance breakers. Then we'll wait."

During this time, Kayla had resumed her pose, which we all tried to ignore.

"So what do you expect to prove by turning the breakers off?"

"Well, I expect to prove or disprove that it is or isn't an appliance.

Then we can move on. In engineering, we call it 'process of elimination'." Now it was my turn to be condescending.

I was actually about to pronounce that it was, in fact, an appliance since we hadn't heard the sound again for a few minutes, when once again, beep...beep...beep. Beep...beep...beep. Beep. . . beep. . . beep.

"It's obviously not an appliance. Now what?" she snapped.

"No, it's not an appliance, but is obviously coming from here in this room, right?" I stated with an edge.

"Well it has to be coming from one of your systems since all my stuff is turned off. And just so you know, I'll be complaining to the manager about this tomorrow."

"You can complain to whomever you like, but that's not going to locate the noise, now is it?" I'd had it up to here with her snot-tude. "As a matter of fact, we're leaving."

I turned to Dave and Jim. "You guys, get your stuff, reinstall the smokes, re-set the breakers and boogey."

"Wait, you can't just leave!"

"Oh, really? Just watch us. It's not in our job description to take verbal abuse from anyone. And I'll guarantee you that sound is not from a building system, so we're outta here." I declared.

Suddenly, a whole new Kayla appeared.

"Okay, okay, I'm sorry. It's just that this has been going on for hours and I can't concentrate on my work or anything."

Yeah right. Work. Must be tough filling in your dance card. I glanced at the calendar which hung on the refrigerator door: *Mike P. Friday, 7:00 PM, Bill M., Saturday, noon.*

I had every intention of walking out when I heard it again. Beep...beep...beep. Beep...beep...beep. Beep...beep...beep.

That's it, damn it! With determination, I went into search and destroy mode. That noise was coming from somewhere in the kitchen and I meant to find it. The whole thing had me ragged off. The sound was familiar, but I couldn't put my finger on it. One thing I was sure of; it wasn't coming from a building system. It was definitely coming from something else.

I began looking in the cabinets, under the sink, even in the garbage can. The real problem was that it wouldn't continue doing it. I was starting with the drawers when it began again.

Beep...beep...beep. Beep...beep...beep. Just as I opened the third drawer: **BEEP...BEEP...BEEP**.

I reached inside and pulled out a pager that was flashing **911** on the screen. It was one of those text message jobs. As I picked it up, I pushed the MESSAGE button and read aloud: "IT'S ME DONALD. I'M REALLY HOT AND I WANT YOU NOW. PLEASE CALL ME ASAP."

Just then, Kayla screamed, "Give me that, you asshole," as she lunged for the pager.

I couldn't resist. As I handed her the pager I said, "Nine-one-one! Jeez. You better call Donald before something bad happens!"

Jim and Dave had turned their faces away and were doing their best to not laugh out loud.

"Shut up, you jerk, and get out! All of you!"

In a deliberately patronizing tone I asked, "Do you want us to replace the smokes and turn on the breakers before we go, ma'am?"

"No. I'll have my friend do it. Just get out!" she fumed.

Friend? Yeah, I bet. Which one? It seemed that there was only one tool old Donny Boy intended to use around Kayla.

"Sure. No problem. But just so you know, there will be a labor charge for all the time we've spent here tonight." It's not nice to be mean to the maintenance guys.

"Fine, whatever -- just leave."

And that was that. No apology, no thank you. So we left.

On the way back to the elevators I said to Jim, "Go to the office and fill out a service request for three man hours to cover this fiasco."

"What should I write down as the reason for the request?"

"Resident reports unknown noise within the apartment - requests assistance."

"How about the resolution?"

I thought about it for a minute as we waited for an elevator to arrive.

"Chief? How 'bout it?"

Finally, my elevator arrived and I stepped in alone. Before the doors closed, I turned and said, "Try this: 'a thorough search of the premises determined that Donald was extremely horny!'"

I returned to my apartment and the crew of *Starship Enterprise*.

Chief engineer's log, supplemental: after having boldly gone where many men have gone before, I am now convinced that there is not, nor will there ever be, intelligent life present in apartment 6211.

Our Engineer Sucks!

It was mid-October and time again for the annual board meeting. The meeting was usually held in a banquet room at one of the Michigan Avenue hotels. It was an affair for yuppies and seniors alike since it was open to all homeowners. Elections were held and reports were given. Free food, free booze, and a lot of complimenting and complaining.

Fortunately for me, the complimenting usually outweighed the complaining by a large margin. So naturally, I looked forward to the affair. It allowed me to take the community pulse, so to speak, and resolve any issues that would affect my annual bonus before December -- and, I must confess, I had developed an unhealthy addiction for ego strokes. My grandfather would have probably said I was getting too big for my britches, but what did he know?

"Hey, Kath, you almost ready?" I called from the living room. It was nearly 6:30 PM and I was getting antsy to head across the street to the Westin. We usually got to the banquet hall about fifteen minutes before the residents to help with the last minute preparations and grab a glass of wine before the meeting started. Kathy has a low tolerance for whiney residents and she always insisted on at least one drink before having to listen to me schmooze.

"Just about," she shouted back. Kathy always got dolled up for this shindig, and it was always worth the wait. She looked good on me and she was sort of a celebrity in her own right. Being a RN as well as the owner of a home health care company, she was asked by the board to administer vaccinations to the residents prior to the flu season each year.

I wish I had a buck for every time a resident told me how lucky I was to have her and a nickel for every time I heard "I can't figure out what she sees in you." Eventually, she came to be known as *Our Nurse Kathy*. I'm pretty sure that most of the residents liked her more than they did me, particularly the old men. Of course, she had an obvious advantage.

"C'mon, Darlin', it's about six-thirty and the pinot is calling!" I was about to go back to the master bedroom when she walked out.

"Nice. I like that. I like it a lot!" She was wearing a business suit -- skirted, naturally. But, wow! At 5'10", thin and blonde with attitude, she stood out in a crowd and made a business suit look sexy. "You look dynamite, Darlin'. Now stay at least an arm's length from Horndog Harris, okay?"

"Oh, Harry. Cut it out," she said as she started to blush. Horndog Harris was about eighty years old, but he was horny just the same, and he always wanted Kathy to take his blood pressure or something. House calls, naturally.

"Let's go." I grabbed her, kissed her and shuffled her out the door.

~~~

While waiting for the elevator, we discussed the meeting. What sort of food they would serve, who would stuff desserts into their oversized purses to take home, etc. Thankfully, when the elevator doors opened, the car was empty. Since the car expressed from sixty-five (my floor) down to forty-four, we were assured that no else would be getting on.

"Now let's try to be tolerant tonight, Darlin'," I said to Kathy as we raced down at 1400 feet per minute. "And if Jane starts glomming onto me, try to remember she's almost seventy and she's the board president, all right?"

"Whatever," she said with a smirk. "I'm sure **somebody** will want to keep me company while you're doing your networking thing."

Before I could give her a comeback, the doors opened onto the 44th floor and we headed to the Sky Lobby and the elevators to the ground floor. Because the bottom half of the building is commercial, the residential portion has a ground floor lobby where the doormen are stationed and a second lobby located on the 44th floor. The two lobbies are connected by three express elevators.

As we waited, I began to feel a bit amorous. I was reaching over to plant a big wet one on Kathy when along comes Mrs. Gentry with her nurse, not so much walking as sashaying.

Mrs. Gentry was a southern belle, born and bred in Podunk, Georgia around the turn of the century, and she was not a woman you wanted to mess with. The day I took over the Hancock she sent word that she "required my presence," so that we might acquaint ourselves. If you think I'm making this up, you're mistaken. You've probably heard of Polk Salad Annie. Mrs. Gentry was her granny. The gators didn't get her. She got them!

"Mr. Budge. Are you going to attend the function this evening?"

"Yes, ma'am, I am. How about you?"

"Well, where else on earth would I be going at this time of night -- the old folks' home, perhaps?"

"No, ma'am, I'm, sorry. I..."

"Yes, I can see that. Oh. I apologize, dear. I didn't see you standing there."

She was addressing Kathy at that point.

"Will you be administering influenza vaccinations this year, dear? If you are, may my caregiver have one? You know I'm concerned, with all the people she comes in contact with. blah, blah, blah." Thankfully, an elevator gong sounded, the doors opened and we all boarded before I nodded off.

When we arrived at the banquet room, things were in order. The buffet tables were set up, but no food was present. The rule was no food until everyone was subjected to all the reports and speeches. As I was surveying the crowd, I noticed the manager, Alan Kane, looking quite bored and trying to be unnoticeable in a corner of the room.

I said to Kathy, "Hey Darlin', let's go say hello to Alan. He looks positively ecstatic." Then we headed over to commiserate.

As we approached, Alan said with a grin, "Looks like the snowbirds are just about all here to fatten up for the trip south. Hi, Kathy, you look radiant as always." Alan, like Kathy, had a low tolerance for these soirées.

"Why, thank you, Alan. What's on this year's agenda? Any engrossing bar graph presentations on the growth of the Association's investments? I'm all aquiver with anticipation," she said, while rolling her eyes.

"No, but I hear that Jane has a humdinger of a speech. And I'm thinking she's going to ask you to give a presentation on the benefits of wheat bran for the digestive tract," he said with a laugh.

Our conversation continued as we watched the residents enter the banquet hall and commented on our separate encounters with each one.

"Rivers was in threatening another lawsuit yesterday," said Alan. Rivers was a tireless complainer and a world class jerk.

"Oh, really?" I said. "Did he remind you that he pays your salary?"

"Nah. He did mention that he thought you should be fired, though. He thinks you're too cocky."

"He must have been checking me out at the fitness center again," I shot back as I grabbed my crotch.

"Harry, you're disgusting!" Kathy exclaimed.

"Not as disgusting as that!" I said, as I nodded toward the door.

Alan and Kathy followed my gaze toward the door. Strutting in was Horndog Harris with a twenty-something redhead on his arm. The faux leopard skirt she wore could have been better described as a belt. And Ol' Horndog couldn't have looked prouder.

"Maybe she's his daughter," Kathy politely offered.

"More likely his nurse," laughed Alan.

"Looks like you've been replaced, Darlin'," I said. "Traded in for a younger model, apparently."

"I wouldn't be surprised if the old fart is dead by morning," Kathy muttered.

We carried on like that for about a half hour or so until Jane, the president of the Board, asked for everyone to take their seats.

"Attention everyone: we have a rather long agenda this evening so we would like to get started." Her hair was a stunning blue and her evening gown was a glittering shade of gold. I was reminded of my Navy days.

"I'd like to remind everyone that immediately following the presentations, drinks and appetizers will be served. So please wait until all the reports have been presented before leaving the meeting."

Well, that was the only way to get everyone to listen to the officers blow their own horns. As the meeting progressed, the lawyers would count all the votes for board members and announce the results at the end. Nobody really gave a crap about the elections. Most people came for the free food and booze. One year, the catering staff made the mistake of setting out the food about halfway through the meeting. That's when the trouble started. The way the old folks started shoving you'd have thought they were giving away Cadillacs. The over-sized Louis Vuitton totes doubled as doggie bags. After that, the rule was no food until everyone was subjected to all the reports and speeches. After about an hour-long procession of boring reports, the last presentation was finally underway.

". . . and here, if we follow the graph, we can see that our reserves have grown by an average of 2.3% over the last year. With the exception of the Smith Barney Mutual Fund which did not perform quite as well as expected, all the other investments have... yada...yada...yada." Jack Henderson, the treasurer droned on and on.

"If he doesn't shut up soon so we can eat, I'm going to gnaw my own arm off," Kathy whispered to me. Like I said before, low tolerance, particularly when she was hungry.

"And so, in conclusion, the Association's financial status is secure and healthy."

And so, the business portion of the annual meeting concluded. Time to party!

~~~

"Let the feast begin," exclaimed Jane from the podium as the cattle raced to the trough.

My mind began replaying images of a soccer match in Britain where ninety or so people were killed when some sympathetic security guards made the mistake of opening the gates to accommodate fans who were not fortunate enough to obtain tickets for seats in the stands. Like lemmings, everyone rushed through the gates, with those behind pushing those in front until confronted by a chain link fence some twenty feet high. The sheer volume of thousands of bodies pushing forward simply crushed the life out of those at the head of the mob. Gruesome.

Although Kathy, Alan and I had briefly considered making a strategic move toward the buffet, we were detained by Stan Lavine, the president of the management company, who requested that we convey his "sincerest" apologies for being required to attend yet another board meeting at another building. Yeah, right Stan. You used that excuse last year, I thought to myself. Whatever. Thankfully, fate/Stan had intervened and our lives were spared.

༄༄༄

"The food is wonderful as usual," Alan said to Jane, who arrived at our table just as we three were sitting down to eat.

"Yes. They always provide the best for us here," Jane answered. "And as usual, the desserts are simply exquisite. Don't you agree, Karen?" Jane said to Kathy, who did her best to brush off what she considered a deliberate snub. (Jane called her something different every time they met.)

"Actually, I thought the berry tarts seemed a bit runny this year." This was Kathy's not so subtle comeback, but it rolled off Jane like water off a duck's butt.

"Really? I must speak to the chef before the night is over. But in the meantime, Harry, I would like to introduce you to some of the residents you may not have met yet. Please excuse us, dear. Alan." And so, I was dragged away from my plate as Kathy and Alan wrinkled their noses and smirked.

"This is Mr. And Mrs. Lange from apartment 8506. And this is Harry Budge, our chief engineer," Jane said as we all shook hands.

"Harry keeps us all safe and happy. And he does it economically as well. In fact, last year he came in nearly 9 percent under budget, etc., etc., etc."

The Langes were about the sixth new couple Jane had paraded me before and I had gotten quite good at accepting the praise. I mean, it was a regular Harry-fest and I was really digging the attention.

"Oh, Harry dear, there's Mrs. Adonomos. We simply must go and say hello," she insisted.

All right, here's Mrs. Adonomos' story. About ninety-eight years old, wheelchair bound, born in Croatia, survivor of seven husbands, richer than God, and really cranky. In addition, she wore glasses made from old telescopes and suffered from Alzheimer's. Of course, we weren't really sure about the Alzheimer's, but she easily forgot inconvenient details. This could be verified by the bookkeeper, since she never failed to dispute a repair charge, claiming that no one had ever come to her apartment to repair anything. Her caregiver apparently suffered a similar affliction since she could never remember anything either.

I'd had a run-in with Mrs. A. early in my tenure, during a reconstruction project to repair the domestic water tank. The tank is located on the same floor as her apartment and the work was extremely noisy. She complained daily and I would be forced to explain to her that the work would have to carry on and that there was nothing to be done. I suppose repeating myself every day eventually made me kinda grouchy and it probably showed.

OUR ENGINEER SUCKS!

Needless to say, she wasn't the friendliest old girl, but somehow I had managed to get on her good side by relieving a service charge or something in the past. She usually nodded when she saw me now. Sometimes, she actually smiled. The last few times I saw her she had even acknowledged my greetings with a wave.

Sitting in her wheelchair, she exuded an air of regal grandeur. Like a queen on a throne, holding court, what with her red velvet dress and a dozen or so residents paying homage. At that time I noticed Kathy and Alan had also wandered over, presumably to whisk me away for a drink.

That was when Jane started her spiel. "Hello, Monica. How are you this evening?" One had to be at least seventy to address Mrs. A. by her first name.

"Ighm dooghink fine," she said, matter-of-factly. "Sank you."

"Well you look marvelous. Monica, you remember Harry Budge, our chief engineer. He's really the best thing that has ever happened to our association. We just don't know what we would do without him," Jane extolled.

"Ogh, rrreally," said Mrs. A. as she scoped me out from head to toe; through her Coke bottle glasses which made her eyes appear to be the size of silver dollars.

I felt my chest start to swell as I reached out for her hand. I mean, I'm only human. As she took it, she pulled me down to look me squarely in the eyes. After a moment, while still grasping my hand she stated quite loudly, in her thick, Eastern European accent, "Vell, Igh surrrely hope you arrr betterrr zen ze von ve have now, becuss zis guy," she sighed and shook her head, "he rrreally sucks!"

I was speechless.

Then, from behind me: "I just hope he can fix the toilet so I don't have to jiggle the handle every time I flush it," I heard Kathy snicker to Alan.

It was there and then, amidst the gasps and the giggles that I realized my grandfather was a genuine sage and I should have paid his counsel a bit more respect. Pride, it seems, really does come before a fall!

Mrs. Cosentino and the Whatcha-ma-call-it

About two weeks had passed since the annual board meeting but I was still kinda salty over the "Our Guy Sucks" episode. I was tiring of the jokes and gibes from the residents as well as the crew.

It was Monday morning and as I entered the management office I noticed that Mandy, the service coordinator, whose I.Q. rivaled that of an African dung beetle, and Lisa the assistant manager, were cracking themselves up about something until they saw me coming. Naturally, I figured I would be the target of yet another lame joke.

"So? What's up?" I asked.

"Oh, nothing," said Mandy in a higher than usual pitch, which meant that something was indeed "up".

"Well then, what's so funny?"

"Not a thing," said Lisa, trying to hold back a laugh.

"You chicks are weird," I stated as I picked up the service requests and began to thumb through them.

Out of the corner of my eye, I noticed that they were both checking me out while trying to appear preoccupied.

Eventually, I came to what I immediately recognized as the source of their glee. A service request had been written for apartment 8808. It read:

> Mrs. Cosentino requests that Harry call to set an appointment to teach her how to use her new food processor.

"Very funny," I said. "You guys are wearing it out." Then I began to tear up the service request.

"Hey, that's real!" exclaimed Lisa.

"You've got to be kidding!" I said.

"Nope," said Mandy, "she just called it in not five minutes ago." She could barely contain herself.

I felt my face start to flush. It's an embarrassing trait. I never could control and it and it telegraphs my emotions like a billboard. They knew they had me.

"Listen, I'm the Chief Engineer for God's sake, not the Chef Engineer."

"Aren't you the one who's always blabbing about how we're a *full service building?*" quipped Lisa sarcastically.

"Maybe, little old ladies just aren't worthy of your attention anymore," chimed Mandy. "Mrs. A. obviously doesn't think very highly of your skills."

I knew it! Sooner or later everything came back to that. Build a thousand bridges and nobody notices. But, just let one fall down and your name is Mudd.

"Why can't one of you do it then?"

"We wouldn't want you to file a grievance with the union for us poaching your work, now would we?" Lisa replied, damn near in tears from trying to hold back the laughter.

"Surely, with all your training and experience, you can figure out a simple food processor. I mean you're supposed to be a mechanical genius!" By this time Mandy had lost control and was practically rolling on the floor.

"Yeah, and anyway, she's a great tipper," chortled Lisa.

That's when I knew I was beaten. After nearly twenty-five years of training and experience as a stationary engineer, a little old lady with a stash of two dollar bills could reduce me to Kitchen Boy. So

MRS. COSENTINO AND THE WHATCHA-MA-CALL-IT

I left the office with what remained of my dignity, as the evil twins commenced howling like a pair of hyenas.

༺ ༻

Mrs. Cosentino really was a sweet old lady. She reminded me of a munchkin. She was barely 4'4" tall, redheaded with barely a trace of gray, sharp as a razor and always cheerful. Regardless of what service anyone provided for her, she would tip them with a two-dollar bill. That in itself, of course, is not unique, even though twos are rarer than they used to be. However, her presentation was truly classy. She would ask you to wait by the door as she went to the bedroom. When she returned, she would be carrying a sheet of bills and a pair of sewing scissors. She would then proceed to meticulously cut a single two from the sheet, hand it to you and say something like, "Thank you for your wonderful work, don't spend it all in one place, now." She was ninety-five and had probably been performing this ritual for about seventy years.

Like most old people, she didn't relate too well to inflation. In 1939, two dollars was probably a fortune. But of course, it was the cutting ceremony that made it worth the while. The first time I experienced it, I thought the old girl was senile and was handing out play money. I had never seen money in sheets. But apparently, years ago, it was common for people, particularly the wealthy, to get their money in sheets from the bank. I even heard stories later, about how at Christmas, some rich folks would wrap presents in sheets of ones. Anyway, Mrs. Cosentino was a legend around the building and frankly, like I said, just a really nice old lady. It was for that reason that I swallowed my pride and called her to make an appointment.

Ring. Ring. Ring.

"Hello."

"Hi, Mrs. Cosentino, this is Harry. The girls in the office said that you needed me to come up?"

"Oh yes, dear. My daughter-in-law took me shopping at Marshall Fields and she convinced me to by a food whatcha-ma-call-it."

"You mean a food processor?" I asked, as if I didn't already know.

"Yes, that's it. But, I don't have a clue how to use it and I thought since you are so good with machines and such, that you wouldn't mind showing me how to work it."

"Well, to be honest, I've never used one myself. But I suppose, between the two of us, we could figure it out."

"Why, yes. I think we could. When can you come up, dear?"

"I can be there in about ten minutes," I said. I figured it might go a long way toward restoring my reputation if I hustled up there right away. There wasn't much else going on anyway.

When I arrived at Mrs. Cosentino's place, I knocked and stood back from the door. Mrs. Coz always looked through the peep hole to see who was on the other side before she opened up. She, like Mrs. Newton and many other old people, was somewhat paranoid, I guess.

As I heard her approach the door, she called, "Is that you, Harry?"

"Yes Ma'am," I replied. Then she stepped up on her little stool to look through the peep hole, just to be sure. The sound of scrapping on the floor was a dead giveaway.

She unlocked and opened the door and said, "How nice it is for you to take time out of your busy day to stop by and help out an old lady."

"Not at all, Mrs. Cosentino. It's my pleasure to help you out." By then, I had actually forgotten all about my wounded pride and looked forward to our little diversion.

As I entered the apartment, I had to pass through the entry hall which was adorned with family photos spanning at least three quarters of a century. Pictures of friends and family, children and grandchildren, neighbors and celebrities, were hung on both sides.

I knew from experience that our culinary arts session would not begin before a short commentary on some of the people portrayed on the walls. Without fail, my tour would end before a portrait of a pretty young woman named Dolly.

Dolly was Mrs. Cosentino's youngest daughter. She had died about forty years earlier from choking in a restaurant in New York City. I had heard the story countless times, as told through tearful eyes by Mrs. Cosentino.

"Dolly was the most beautiful girl you would ever lay eyes on," she would say. "She could enchant a man with simply a glance."

Out of respect, I would always listen as if it were the first time I had heard the story. And I wondered if anyone would remember me with such affection after forty years.

Anyway, as predicted, I had my history lesson and then it was time to proceed to the kitchen. As we entered, I immediately focused on the procession of bowls neatly arranged on the counter. At the head of the line was a box, unopened, with a picture of some kind of cooking gadget surrounded by a virtual cornucopia of veggies on the front.

What impressed me most was the fact that every root, tuber, legume, bulb, and fruit depicted on the box was neatly represented in the bowls; in precisely the same order as the photograph. This lady was thorough! If only my engineers were this well organized, I thought, there would probably be a lot less spare parts after a machine repair.

"My, we've been busy," I stated, loudly. Mrs. Cosentino was a bit hard of hearing.

"Well, I just wanted to be prepared," she said.

"So you've never used a food processor?" I asked redundantly. "As I said on the phone, I haven't either unless you count an egg beater."

"No," she said. "My daughter-in-law said that I should learn to use one because it would make my life easier. I told her my life was already quite easy, especially with all of you here to take care of me, and there was nobody around to cook for anyway. But she insisted that this gadget was something that nobody could live without. To be honest, I just gave in so she would stop nagging me."

"Well, then, let's figure this thing out," I replied, as I reached over for the box. Made in China. Hmmm.

"Let's see now, I guess we should open it this way," I mumbled as I tried to open the box. As most men know, getting the box open without destroying it is the trick. I guess I'm a bit anal that way. Kathy calls it OCD, whatever that means.

Naturally, the box would not open easily, but I was determined. After inspection, I discovered the proper order in which to remove tab A from slot B, etc., and got the box opened at one end. That's when the bane of all mechanically inclined individuals presented itself; the Styrofoam nesting cube. You know, that hermetically sealed, white thing that allows five pounds of parts to be packed into a three pound space.

The annoying squeaks which accompany removal of each part make the cubes especially fun to play with. The fact is, I rate these "product protection systems" right up there with *blister packs*. Half the time, you either wreck the product inside while attempting to extricate it or you wind up in the hospital receiving stitches. I believe that both of these packaging methods are China's revenge on the entire Western world for introducing their youth to rock and roll.

Worse even than unpacking something from either of these puzzles was trying to re-pack it. It simply can't be done, which generally prevents the consumer from returning the product. A truly ingenious way to ensure that all sales remain "final!"

Anyway, with clenched teeth, I removed the various parts and laid them on the counter. Then I picked up the instruction book and turned to Mrs. Cosentino.

"Okay. Now, let's take this thing for spin," I said.

"Oh dear -- it looks quite complicated, doesn't it?"

"We'll figure it out. Not to worry," I said, more to reassure myself than to settle her.

I began to read: *While helding you new GEMCO Kitchen Genie base unit in one hand, attach stainless stell cutter A by firmly snapping into place on drives shaft with you other hand.* Something told me that the Anglo-Chinese translator was the same guy who did the number on my electric carving knife instructions.

"Let's see now, which one is stainless steel cutter A?" I asked myself aloud. "Got it!"

"What's that do?" Mrs. Cosentino inquired.

"I'm not sure yet, but let's see."

I attached the cutter to the base unit and plugged it into the receptacle. Now what?

This cutter is intend to slice delicious home-made chips of potato, the instructions read.

"It says we can make potato chips with this one," I told Mrs. Coz.

"Oh, let's try it," she giggled.

I reached for a potato with my right hand. Then I read on. *While firmly helding base unit, gently fed potato into mouth of processing chamber. Chips of potato will come out of outlet at front of unit.* Looks simple, I thought.

"Here goes," I said as I turned on the unit and fed the tater into the mouth.

"Oh look," Mrs. Cosentino cried as a stream of paper thin potato slices shot from the outlet. "Aren't you clever? That is just amazing!" Actually, it was kinda cool.

"Would you like to try?" I asked her.

"I don't think so, just yet. Why don't we try another thingy on the end?"

"All right, then," I replied. "How about this one? The book says it can make waffle fries."

"Oh, yes, let's try that one."

So I grasped the base unit and exchanged attachment A with attachment B. At that point, I didn't think I needed to read the instructions anymore; the pictures would suffice.

True to the pictorial, attachment B produced perfectly formed waffle fries. I gained a whole new respect for Chinese technology. The machine was noisy, but it was delivering. I'd like to see anybody produce a waffle fry like that by hand!

I was getting into it. "Let's try some of the other attachments now. What do you say?" I asked Mrs. Cosentino with enthusiasm.

"Well, all right," she said. "What else can it do?"

"You name it. How 'bout some Julienne carrots?"

"Okay," she said. "If you think so, Harry."

"Let's do it!"

We (I) proceeded to slice and dice everything in sight. About ten pounds of food altogether, I'd say. Change the cutting head - change the shape of the end product. Simple. I had bowls of cucumber slices with ridges, a colander full of French fries of all varieties, a plate full of perfectly sliced tomatoes begging for salt, even a dish of hash browns and onions. We had lemons sliced for iced tea, diced carrots mixed with peas, melon balls -- you name it. And, the pièce-de-resistance...riced potatoes! (Mrs. Coz had already boiled a couple of Idahos during my French fry binge). If only we had eggs!

I'm telling you, this machine had it going on. The old girl kept feeding me the fuel and I kept rockin'. Suddenly though, I realized that Mrs. Cosentino was not so much participating as she was observing.

"I'm sorry, Mrs. Cosentino," I apologized. "It looks like I've carved everything up and you haven't even tried it yet. You got some more spuds or anything?"

"No, I'm sorry. I'm afraid you've used up everything I had."

"Well, I could go home and get some stuff and come back and then you could try it," I offered.

"That's all right, dear. I believe I can do it now. You're a very good instructor. I think we've had enough training for one lesson. You must have a lot of other work to do."

As impressed as I was with the Kitchen Genie, I had been there a while and I did have other things to do. I felt somewhat remorseful for blowing off all that time. But mostly, I felt guilty for hogging up all the fun.

"Well, I do have some things to take care of. But, if you want, I could come back later with some more vegetables and you could try it," I offered again.

"No, really, Harry. I think I can handle it from here now," she insisted. "Anyway, I think you've cut more than enough for today."

"All right, then -- I'll see you later, Mrs. Cosentino," I said as I headed for the door. "At least you won't have to cut up any veggies for awhile," I quipped.

"That's for sure," she agreed. "But, aren't you forgetting something?" she said with a smile. "Wait here. I'll be right back."

I waited by the door, as directed, and of course she returned with a sheet of bills and her trusty scissors. But, to my surprise, she was holding a sheet of fives.

"I save these for special gifts," she said. "You've really earned it this time."

As she began to trim a bill from the sheet, I noticed that there were none missing yet. This must have truly been a special occasion for her. As she handed me the five I thought, see, you've still got it. That old crank Mrs. Adonomos was probably just having an episode. It wasn't like five bucks was going to make me rich, but the gesture did wonders for my battered ego. I couldn't wait to wave that five up under everybody's noses.

"Why, thank you, Mrs. Cosentino. It's not necessary, you know. I really enjoyed learning how to use the watcha-ma call-it with you!"

We both laughed and said goodbye. I left and returned to the office feeling better than I had for days.

The next day I started my routine again, just like I had the day before and the one before that. I went to the office for coffee and to go over the plan of the day with the crew.

As always, we discussed the previous day's work and reviewed the completed work orders, checked the schedule to see which PMs were due for which pieces of equipment, etc. After about a half hour of that and dealing with the personnel issues (vacation requests, so-and-so stole my lunch, Mr. What's-his-butt says he's going to get me fired), I headed to the management office.

Once again, as I entered the office, I could tell that Lisa and

MRS. COSENTINO AND THE WHATCHA-MA-CALL-IT

Mandy were doing the dance. They just couldn't wait to screw with me about Mrs. Cosentino and the food processor. They were such commoners.

"Hey! Check this out," I announced as I started waving my new five around like a pennant. "Harry's got his groove back, oh yeah! This ain't no two-dollar bill either, chiquitas. Noooo. This here is a five, fresh cut from a new sheet, no less. Ha!"

"Ooooh, you must really be the man," said Lisa, with a sarcastic tone of voice.

"Yeah, I'll bet nobody can please a ninety-five-year-old lady like you can," blurted Mandy.

"We're so lucky to have you around, aren't we?" commented Lisa, again with that funky tone. "I'm sure Mrs. Cosentino is looking forward to your next visit," she continued as she started gagging.

"What are you laughing about? I figured that thing out in no time and there ain't nothing like the smell of a brand-new Lincoln," I said as I put the bill to my nose sniffed.

"No doubt, a pity tip," Mandy giggled.

"Yeah, whatever. You two are just jealous," I declared as I picked up the service requests.

As I began thumbing through them, Lisa and Mandy headed for the door, with their hands over their mouths, trying not to choke. Good thing, too. Lisa's laugh was particularly nerdy, like Arnold Horschak's from "Welcome Back Kotter."

No matter, once again, all is right in my world and nothing is gonna bring me down, I said to myself. However, as I scanned the pile, my eyes landed on yet another service request for apartment 8808. No way! I couldn't believe it. But there it was, in black and white.

Mrs. Cosentino requests that Harry stop by to put the food

> *whatcha-ma-call-it back in the box the right way, so she can take it back to Marshall Field's. She says it wastes too much food!*

At that moment I felt as if someone had hit me in the head with a two-by-four. I addition to enduring the sheer agony of repacking the dreaded nesting cube, I would also be subjected to even further ridicule by the twisted sisters. The value of my five dollar bill had suddenly diminished to less than zero. That's when I realized that I was experiencing an epiphany; an unalterable, inescapable fact: *Sometimes, it just sucks to be me!*

Don't Mess with Boomer

Boomer is my cat. Actually, he's my son's cat. Harry wouldn't stop bugging me since that Ulysses deal. His mom wouldn't let him have a kitten, so I decided to get him one for his birthday and keep him at my place.

Kathy found Boomer for me at a country vet's office near her house. He was born in a barn which explains why he is the way he is. As things turned out, Boomer and I ended up roommates, and eventually buddies. That's not to say that the two of us didn't have our occasional spats. One episode in particular defined the parameters of our relationship for many years to come.

Soon after we picked up our little bundle of joy, Kathy and I went on a two-week vacation. Boomer had been neutered and vaccinated but he was too young to have his claws removed at the time. The vet said he would be able to perform the procedure when we returned.

I would always have the guys check on the pets and plants when we traveled. Good thing. Apparently, Boomer had developed an obsession with sharpening his claws on my new leather living room set while we were gone. The unanimous decision by the crew was to cover the entire set with cardboard and duct tape. I was pissed when we first walked in because all I wanted to do was get horizontal and watch TV; not spend a half hour uncrating the furniture. But after I saw the damage he had already inflicted, I was grateful for the crew's diligence. Shortly after that, Master Boomer lost all his little shredders. I did allow him to retain his teeth however, which in retrospect may have been a questionable decision.

I was under the impression that neutering a male cat would make him more docile and affectionate. Well, if that's true, it didn't take with Boomer. He got into everything when he was young, just like that little shit, Ulysses. Kathy and I once looked for him for twenty minutes before leaving for the airport. Eventually, we found him in a dresser drawer. His muffled cries had finally led us to his makeshift nest of bras and underwear.

He could also be incredibly annoying at times. You could start out playing an innocent game with him, say, with a ball of twine or something and sooner or later, he would take a dive at you, bite and run away. But like a kid, he didn't like being ignored for very long. In time, he'd sneak up and nip your leg or something to get your attention.

Another thing -- right out of the clear blue sky, he'd start running around the apartment jumping from chairs to tables and bounce off the walls like a pinball. When he finally stopped, he would look over his shoulder, right at you, as if to say, "How'd ya like that?"

Many times when I came home from work, he would be sitting in my lounge chair, like an old man, with his back against the back of the chair, watching TV (I usually left the tube on during the day to amuse him). I've never seen any other cat sit that way in my life. Once, I put a bottle of beer in front of him and took a photo to use on my Christmas cards.

All this was entertaining at first. But as time went on, he started getting more and more territorial. Not vicious or anything. He would just let everyone know who was in charge in the condo. Whenever a guest would enter, the first thing he would do was the normal cat thing. You know, rub all over your legs and cover you with hair and roll around on his back. Then he'd jump up, nip at you and run away while looking over his shoulder, as if daring you to chase him. Boomer wasn't biased. He'd pull that crap on me, too.

Well, one weekend, Kathy's two oldest boys, Luke and Matt, were on spring break from college and wanted to visit the city with their girlfriends. Naturally, they stayed with me.

They all knew Boomer from previous visits. The girls were afraid of him, but the guys always loved to screw with him. Matt was the worst. He'd always start messing with Boomer the way he did with his younger brother, Marc. Everything would start out as fun, but would end up with somebody, in Matt's words, "getting all serious." Before you knew it, someone was either crying or pissed off and the situation would require an intervention. The only difference between Marc and Boomer was that Boomer wouldn't cry; he'd bite.

This particular weekend, when the kids showed up, we all sat down and had a drink and discussed what was going on in their lives at school, their jobs, etc. They wanted to go hang out at Rush and Division, where all the bars and clubs were. So, while the girls went to the bathrooms to get themselves dolled up, the boys and I continued drinking and talking.

True to form, Matt got bored and started antagonizing Boomer. And just like Marc, Boomer would keep coming back for more. I yelled at Matt a couple of times to "leave the cat alone," but Boomer would keep sneaking back to bite him one last time when he wasn't looking.

That's when I got the bright idea to get out the bullwhip I had gotten for Harry when I visited my sister in Phoenix. I knew from experience that Boomer hated the sound the whip made when I snapped it. He would run and hide under the table when he heard the crack and make the most God-awful sound you ever heard, like a cross between a growl and a whine. Luke and Matt thought it was pretty funny. Boomer didn't think so at all.

"This is how you tame a lion," I said. I guess inside every man, regardless of age, dwells an idiot. All it takes is the proper amount of alcohol to release his latent stupidity.

"I am master of this domain," I proclaimed, as I cracked the whip, following Boomer from one hiding place to another. He finally dashed behind the couch as the girls announced they were ready to go.

"You guys are a bunch of cruel morons!" stated Luke's girl, Erin, as she walked into the room. "No wonder he's so aggressive." I think she was some kind of psych major or something.

"Hey, you have to teach an animal who's boss," I told her.

"Whatever," she said with the accent on **ever**, like young girls do.

"Well, let's go, you guys," said Luke, and the four of them headed for the door.

⁂

After they all left I figured it was time to make up with Boomer and get him settled down. So I went over to the couch and tried to coax him out.

"Grrrrr." He wasn't going for it. I guess he was still pissed.

"Come on out, boy. Matt's gone and I put the whip away," I said in a quiet voice. But he started that hideous crying/growling thing again. So then I made the mistake of reaching behind the couch to get him.

Man, that was definitely the wrong thing to do. He chomped on my hand, hard. When I withdrew, I was bleeding from four little puncture wounds.

That really set me off. I should have just let him be. But, noooo! Just like the moron Erin said I was, I got the bullwhip out again and started cracking it in his direction. Boomer continued his nasty growl thing, but, he wouldn't come out.

So then I got the broom and started trying to force him out the other side. Next, he started gnawing on the broom stick while making that funky sound.

Finally, he ran out the other side and settled behind a fichus tree in the corner. I laid down the broom and approached the corner where he was crouching, making that gruesome noise.

"I told you before, I don't go for that biting bullshit," I snapped as I reached for the scruff of his neck. That's when he bit me on the forearm, like a cougar. I smacked him with my other hand and he went flying through the fichus tree, which fell over, spilling dirt everywhere.

"Shit. You little bastard! I'm gonna kick your ass," I screamed as he ran to a new hiding place.

I was now bleeding pretty badly from the bites, plus there was a huge mess on the floor. Obviously, the situation was getting out of hand.

"I'm not done with you yet," I yelled at Boomer as I poured another scotch. Of course getting drunker would definitely improve my judgment as well as my attitude.

Here I present the reader with living proof that you can't argue with a drunk. Any sober person would have just let the stupid cat settle down on his own and that would have been the end of it. But, not this time. I was sick and tired of that little prick biting everybody all the time and acting like he owned the place. I made my mind up that I was going to teach Mr. Boomer who was in charge, once and for all.

I had one more drink for good measure, and set my plan in motion. After I located the ornery little shit, under an end table, I closed the doors to the bedrooms and the kitchen. That was step one. Then I grabbed my trusty bullwhip and herded him into the guest bath where I kept his litter box. After all, he'd need it when I was done with him. As I closed the door, he jumped into the bath tub.

"I've got you now, spinkter boy," I told him. That's when all hell broke loose.

I reached down with my left hand to grab him and he chomped down on it like a pit bull. As I shrieked in pain and swung at him with my open right hand, he tore his teeth through my left forefinger, down to the bone. When he finally ripped through, he immediately turned, and bit down through the web of flesh between my right thumb and forefinger.

Now both my hands were bleeding profusely and my rage was out of control. I smacked him with my mangled left hand and aimed a punch at his head with my right. But, in mid-swing, he dodged and my fist slammed into the top edge of the tub. Based on the pain, I knew I had broken something.

There was blood everywhere and Boomer still didn't have a scratch on him. I lost it. With the speed of a cobra, I grabbed him by the throat with my bloody left hand. He couldn't bite anymore, but he instinctively tried to scratch me with his clawless rear paws.

"You think you can bite me and get away with it, asshole?" I screamed.

The more he tried to scratch the tighter I squeezed. Before long however, I realized that I was close to strangling him. I blinked a couple of times before I released my grip and dropped him into the tub. After a moment, I turned on the shower, as much to cool myself off as to revive Boomer. The rumble was over.

We both laid in the tub, panting, under the shower, which was mixing water with my blood and matting down his hair. I was bleeding all over the place and Boomer started making that disgusting growling/crying sound, only with a lot less enthusiasm. I finally decided to do what I should have done in the first place: *leave him alone.*

I stood up, turned off the shower, and stepped over to the sink to review my injuries. Left forefinger: shredded and requiring stitches. Right forearm: bleeding from puncture wounds. Right hand: several deep lacerations and a probable broken middle finger.

I wrapped my wounds as best I could and went to bed; leaving Boomer, whining in the tub. It must have been several hours later that Luke was shaking me to wake me up.

"Harry, are you all right?" he asked.

"What did you say?" I was still half asleep.

"There's blood all over the bathroom and the girls are freaking out," he said.

"Oh yeah, it's nothing. Just go to bed," I replied and rolled over.

"You sure?"

"Yeah, yeah, I'm cool. Just go and crash," I insisted.

When morning rolled around I awoke with incredible pain in both my hands and a vicious hangover. I also realized I would have some '*splainin*' to do. The kids were still asleep so I entered the guest bath where the fight had ensued between Boomer and me. Sure enough, there were blood stains all over the place. I took some Tylenol and proceeded to clean up the mess with my mangled hands. Then I went to look for Boomer.

"Boomer," I called. "Come out and get some Meow Mix." At that point, I'm not sure what was hurting worse, my hands, my head, or my conscience.

"C'mon boy, let's make up."

Still nothing.

"C'mon. I'm sorry, dude."

As I neared the recliner we normally shared I heard a whole new sound. To this day, it defies description. It was coming from under the chair. Instinctively, I knew it was Boomer. Somehow, he had gotten inside the bottom of the chair. Every time I spoke he made that creepy sound.

I considered lifting the foot rest, but, being an engineer, I knew that the scissors mechanism could seriously injure him if he was lying in it. Furthermore, I was a bit leery of tangling with him again after the night before. I mean, c'mon. He really jacked me up! So I wisely decided to leave him be.

———

By the time the kids began to stir I was already on my third cup of coffee, my second dose of Tylenol, and about halfway through the Sunday crossword puzzle, my pen held in my bulbous bandaged fist. As usual, Luke was the first one up.

"Harry, what the heck happened last night, anyway?"

"Boomer and I had a disagreement," I stated casually.

"Disagreement!" He was incredulous. "The bathroom looked like a combat zone when we got home last night!"

"Well, things got a little out of hand after you guys left."

"Yeah, I can see that," he stated as he pointed at my bandaged hands.

"Well, you guys got Boomer all wound up and this is the result," I said.

"Hey, Matt's the one that got him riled! And he wasn't that bad 'till you started going all Indiana Jones and shit."

"Shut up, Luke. I told you guys before not to bother him, didn't

I? You want some coffee, or what?"

"Sounds good. Where's he at now?" he asked as I handed him a cup.

"He's under the recliner and if you know what's good for you, you won't mess with him," I stated.

Just then, Matt stumbled out of the guest room. "Hey Harry, the bathroom looked like the ER last night. What gives?"

So then I had to start the whole story over, which I was destined to do twice again over the course of the morning. Naturally, the girls were appalled and the guys just thought the whole thing was awesomely hilarious, considering my hands were bandaged up like boxing gloves. The whole time, Boomer remained in his hiding place, occasionally vocalizing with that weird growling sound. At least the kids left him alone.

I did the best I could to serve breakfast, while listening to the kids recount their adventures on Rush Street. Afterward, everybody packed their stuff and got ready to go. On their way out the door, as if on cue, Kathy called.

"Wait a minute Hon, the kids are just leaving."

While saying goodbye to the kids, with the phone to my ear, Matt shouted, "Hey, Mom. Harry got his butt kicked last night!"

"What!" Kathy snapped in my ear.

"Nothing, Darlin'," I said into the phone.

Then to Matt, "Thanks a lot, jag-bag. Now get lost. Drive safely and come back again when you can't stay so long."

As I closed the door I heard him tell the others, "Harry's gonna get it."

Then from the receiver in my hand, "Harry Budge, what did they mean you got your butt kicked? Did you go out with them and get stupid last night?"

"No, I never went anywhere." Then I proceeded to recount the entire saga for the fifth time.

"You are such an idiot," she said when I finished. "You're a grown man and you're supposed to set an example. Getting drunk and fighting with the cat. That's real smart," blah, blah, blah.

After about a half hour of being lectured to and not one iota of sympathy, I finally said, "Okay, now that I know how much you care, can I get started cleaning up my place?"

"Whatever. Just don't expect me to feel sorry for you if you end up in the hospital with an infection. You deserve it. And you better just hope no one turns you in to the Anti-cruelty Society. It would serve you right."

"10-4. Got it. Catch ya later."

I hung up. My hands were killing me, the place was a mess and I was concerned for Boomer. Besides, I couldn't take any more criticism, no matter how "constructive."

I puttered around the apartment, picking up and putting things away, trying to ignore the pain in my hands. Occasionally, I would go over to the recliner and say something like "Hey Boomer, c'mon out and get some food," or "Hey, buddy, wanna make up?" But he wasn't going for any of it. He'd just make that hideous sound. So finally, I decided all I could do was leave him be.

I hung around and watched TV for the remainder of the day and took Tylenol at the shortest possible intervals. After a while though, it didn't really help.

I re-inspected and cleaned my wounds. They were pretty bad and I should have gone to the hospital for stitches but I didn't fancy the thought of relating the story again in the emergency room. I could just imagine the disdain I would encounter.

So I got a needle and thread and some peroxide and sewed the worst of the gashes closed. I had sewn up minor cuts on myself and others before. It's not much different from sewing cloth, really, except that it hurts like a bitch. The end product isn't pretty, but it works if you don't care much about scarring.

When I was done with the stitching, I sprayed on some of that liquid skin stuff. Then I wrapped the whole works with some gauze and tape and that was that.

Of course when I told Kathy later about my self-administered first aid, I got another lecture about unsanitary this and infection that and how I would probably get cat scratch fever, etc. Finally, I'd had enough so I said goodnight and went to the bedroom and crashed.

When Monday morning rolled around my wake-up call from Kathy went pretty much the way I expected it would.

"How's your hands, Tarzan?" she asked as I answered the phone.

"Not bad," I lied. They were throbbing.

"Well don't come crying to me if you have to have them amputated." Have I mentioned Kathy's compassionate bedside manner?

"Whatever. I won't bother you with my injuries. I'm sure I'll survive without your tender loving care."

"We'll see, tough guy. What are you going to tell everybody at work when they ask you what happened?"

"Why don't you just let me worry about that, all right?"

"Okay," she said in that higher than normal pitch that really means, "I'm smarter than you and you're gonna see."

"Hey, I gotta go. Love you. I'll talk to you later."

"Love you too, bye."

Predictably, I had to relate the story a dozen more times. The guys had a million jokes. You know, like, "Harry's lion took him for a walk on the wild side," or "In this corner we have Boomer the Bad-Ass

Bengal and in this corner we have Harry the Real Meal Budge," or my personal favorite, "When Animals Attack : The Boomer Edition." You get the picture.

I made it through the day and went home to relax and to see if Boomer was ready to make up.

When I arrived at the apartment, I cracked a beer and sat down in the recliner. I called out to Boomer, but got no response. I resisted the urge to go poking around, looking for him. Instead, I decided to stretch out on the couch and watch some TV.

After a while, I noticed Boomer, sort of slinking out from behind the recliner, with his ears back and his belly close to the floor. Man, did he look like shit! His fur was all matted down and bloodstained. I said something to him, but he just made a whining sound and kept his distance. I tried to ignore him, but I kept checking him out from the corner of my eye. I half expected some kind of sneak attack. But we passed the rest of the evening without interaction. Finally, I went to bed.

It was a few days later that the two of us took our first small step toward reconciliation. I was in my usual position, stretched out, watching Star Trek, when Boomer came over and jumped up on the back of the couch. He looked a lot better since he'd cleaned himself up. As he settled himself into a position above my head I instinctively reached up to pet him, but he jumped back and hissed. I figured it was all about little steps.

I ignored him for the rest of the evening. He remained on his perch, but flinched whenever I moved. Eventually, Boomer worked his way back to his lair behind the recliner and I went to bed.

As the days and weeks passed, little by little, my wounds healed, as did my relationship with Boomer.

One day, he just jumped up next to me on the couch, the way he used to. Before long he was purring and asleep. If not for the scars and the various pains in my fingers, I'd have said we were back to normal.

I reflected on the incident frequently over the next several months. I was having trouble assuaging my guilt and embarrassment over the entire episode. I grew up believing a person should learn from his mistakes. There should be some sort of lesson.

The moral eluded me until one day in late October while I was assisting Kathy's father perform a repair on one of his old John Deere tractors. Having descended from a long line of family farmers dating back to the eighteen-forties, Myron Stackhouse is a veritable common sense dispenser.

"What's the problem?" he asked when he noticed me wincing as I used a ratchet wrench to tighten a bolt with my right hand.

"Aw, it's nothing, just a little pain left over from that altercation I had with Boomer back in the spring," I replied.

"Hmmm. You mean that time you got all drunked up and decided to teach the cat a lesson?"

"Uh, yeah, that time," I answered, trying to ignore the rebuff more than the pain. Of course everybody knew the entire story, front to back, courtesy of Kathy and her boys.

"So, did you learn anything from the experience?" he asked me in his folksy, country drawl.

"Well, I'm sure there's a lesson in there somewhere, but I haven't quite nailed it down yet--I'm still working on it," I answered, as I continued back and forth with the ratchet.

"Is that a fact? I'd have thought that a smart city fella like you would have had it all figured out by now," he said without malice. "Why, it's something every farm boy learns as soon as he can walk."

After about thirty seconds, with the only sound between us being the cricket-like chirping of the ratchet; click, click, click, click, click …click, click, click, click, click…click, click, click, click, click…the suspense finally got to me.

"Well? What?" I asked, sort of indignantly, as I looked up and stopped wrenching.

With a mischievous grin and a tone of conviction, he looked me in the eye and flatly stated: <u>Never, ever, mess with anything that was born in a barn. Especially when ya been drinkin'!</u>"

9/11

Here come old flat top, he come groovin' up slowly…right over left,
He got ju-ju eyeballs …wrap around,
He shoot coca cola…down through the middle,
He got hair down to his knees…around the front,
*Got to be good lookin' 'cause he's so hard to see…*up through the middle,
Come together, right now, over me. Down through the front once more and, voilà!

It's funny, the things you remember and the things you forget. I didn't wear a tie very often, so I usually had to make more than one attempt at tying it. When I did wear one, there was an important reason.

I remember standing in front of the mirror, tying my tie, while jammin' to that Beatles tune playing on the radio. It's an earworm. It sounds good no matter what. You hear it once and you're singing it in your head for days. It happens to everybody. I can remember that, but I can't remember the reason I chose to wear a tie that day. Like I said, it's kinda funny.

"It looks like it's going to be a beautiful day today here. How is it there?" Kathy asked. She had just called me for our morning phone conversation as I was getting ready for work. Kathy figured it was her duty to make sure I was up and getting ready for work on time. You know, having three sons and all. Anyway, I was done with the tie and looked somewhat professional.

"Yeah, it looks good here too," I said as I looked out over the city. Cranes and derricks were standing tall in every direction, symbols of the residential construction wave that was engulfing the downtown area. What a great city, what a great place to live. I felt as if I was on top of the world. I had a great job, a great girl, an awesome pad. I'd sure come a long way from the south side.

I turned on the TV as we continued talking. The Today Show was on. It was about a quarter to eight and Matt Lauer was doing some story which was interesting at the time, but I can't remember now what it was about.

Suddenly, the picture was replaced by that screen that comes up when there is a breaking story. Then, Matt was back and stuttered something about a plane hitting the north tower of the World Trade Center. The picture then shifted to a shot of the tower with a smoking hole in its side about ten or twenty stories from the top.

"Jesus, Kathy! An airplane just crashed into the World Trade Center," I said.

"What?" she asked. She was in her car so she had no idea what I was talking about.

"A plane just slammed into the World Trade Center!" I exclaimed again.

"You mean, like a little private plane, or what?" she asked.

"I don't know, but it sure did some damage. There's a ginormous hole in the side with fire coming out of it."

"Well, what caused it to crash?" Kathy asked.

"I have no idea, hold on a second," I said. "Matt's back on, so is Katie."

"It appears that a commercial jetliner has crashed into the north tower of the World Trade Center. At this time we have no further information other than the tower is on fire as can be seen from all over Manhattan."

Then there was a live shot again of the tower with black smoke billowing out of the side.

"Man, Kathy. You should see this. It's burning pretty bad. They just said it was a commercial jet. I don't get how a pilot could not see a skyscraper in his way."

We kept talking about it for a few more minutes. It was about eight and I needed to get to work. I was about to tell Kathy goodbye when suddenly, right before my eyes, another plane slammed into the other tower. And there was no question about the size of that one. It was huge. This shot was live since there was already news cameras focused on the first crash.

"Holy shit! You're not gonna believe this," I shouted into the phone. "Now, another plane just crashed into the other tower!"

"You're kidding, right?"

"No, I'm not kidding. There must be a problem with the air traffic controllers at JFK or something!"

After another moment of discussion, I said, "I'm late, Darlin'. I gotta go. I'll call you later, okay?"

"All right -- I love you," said Kathy.

"Love you too. Bye."

In the elevator, on the way down, I considered what I had seen on TV. What the hell was going on? One plane crashing into a building is weird, but two planes crashing into adjacent skyscrapers... that's incredible! At that point I never suspected anything evil. It was simply some kind of horrific accident, albeit, one of immense proportions.

When I got to the office, the guys were all standing around talking about nothing, as usual.

"Morning, chief," said Clemente as I entered, in his usual upbeat manner. The guy was always smiling. Frankly, I don't think you could make him frown if you kicked him in the gonads.

"Good morning, Clemente. Hey, did you guys hear what happened to the Trade Center in New York?" I asked.

Fred, my assistant said, "I heard something on the radio about a plane crashing into one of the buildings."

"Actually, another one just hit the other tower, too," I stated.

"What do think caused it, chief?" one of the guys asked.

"I don't know. Maybe an air traffic control screw-up at JFK."

"Hey, remember when those Arabs tried to blow up the one tower back in the early nineties?" Steve blurted out.

"Yeah, but it didn't work. Those buildings were built to last forever. Just like this one." I remember thinking: Yeah, we know how to build skyscrapers in this country.

We talked a little more, finished coffee, and then got on with it.

"Fred, let's go down to street level and check things out. The driveway project is starting on Monday," I said. "I don't want anything to delay us." We had been planning the resurfacing project for months.

Fred and I headed toward the elevators and the rest of the guys went on their way.

"Before we head down, I want to stop at my place and see what's going on with the news." I had left the TV on when I came down to the office. Fred pushed the "up" button.

When we walked in, Boomer started his rubbing routine all over Fred. I went over to the living room with Fred and Boomer in tow. There on the screen was a shot of both towers smoldering. Matt Lauer's voice was dubbing over the live shot.

"... and every emergency service in the city has been activated. Hundreds of firefighters are on the scene. There have been reports of people jumping from windows to escape the intense heat..."

"You see that, man?" I couldn't believe it. Both towers were smoking. After a couple of minutes of watching and commenting I said, "Let's go. I want to see Alan on the way down."

"Morning," I said as we entered Alan's office. He was turning on the TV which we used to monitor the cable service in the building. There they were, both towers of The World Trade Center, belching black smoke. We were mesmerized by the scene on the TV. It was about 8:55 AM.

Suddenly, without warning, the south tower began to collapse. The antennae sort of leaned a bit and then the whole building began to pancake down on itself. From start to finish, I bet it took less than a minute. Then there was something like a mushroom cloud and it was over.

"The south tower of the World Trade Center has just collapsed," I heard the newscaster say incredulously.

"Christ almighty! Did you guys see that?" I shouted.

Fred said, "It looks like what happens when they blow up those old brick buildings."

"Yeah, an implosion," I stated. "Only, they don't do it with buildings that tall." I didn't think anything could have brought down a skyscraper the likes of the World Trade Center.

"Man, that's messed up," was all Fred had left to say.

Then, from the newscaster, *"This just in, a commercial jetliner has just crashed into the Pentagon..."*

"What the hell is going on?" I asked rhetorically. "Is our whole air traffic control system out, or what?"

"Something tells me it's more than that," said Alan.

"Maybe. Whatever, we still have a building to run, so let's get on with it. Alan I'll catch you later, maybe some lunch at Ditka's, all right?"

"Yeah, we'll see," he said as Fred and I left. Although the Trade Center incident was fascinating, in a morbid sense, I really didn't have the time to hang around and gawk at the TV. There was business that needed attending to. Little did I know then that my priorities were about to change.

Fred and I headed down to the Delaware lobby. We walked outside still talking about the plane crashes.

"Man, I ain't never seen nothing like that," said Fred as we walked through the revolving door.

"Me neither," I replied. "I can't believe that tower came down. I bet a lot of people died in that building. The people above the fire didn't have a prayer."

"No way. They said people were jumping out the windows."

"Don't forget about the Pentagon."

It was still sunny and warm outside. I sat on one of the planters and reached for a cigarette. As I lit up I said to Fred, "We need to get the construction barriers ready for Monday. Get some of the guys and move the saw horses down to the helix."

The helix is the double spiral ramp which winds up to the garage entrance on the sixth floor. At the base are two store rooms where residents store bicycles and we store equipment.

"All right," he acknowledged.

We talked a little more about work and the Trade Center and the Pentagon as I finished my smoke and then we headed back into the building and back up to 44. I returned to my office and Fred went about his business.

When I got to the office, I checked my voice mail, fired up my computer, and grabbed a cup of coffee. Then I settled down for what was one of my least favorite tasks - checking email. God, I detest email. Why couldn't people simply call you on the phone, or tell you things in person?

My keyboard skills are of the tried but true hunt-and-peck style, and I soon get irritated. The majority of my email is of the "get Viagra on line" or "enlarge your penis" or "check me out on my web-cam" variety. Unfortunately, important messages get sandwiched in between the spam so a guy has to be careful not to delete the ones that matter.

It wasn't long before my two index fingers had had enough. Fred entered the office and stated, "All the horses are downstairs and ready to go. You hear anything else about the Trade Center?"

"Nah. I've been playing with the computer since I got here. You want to stop by my place and see what's going on?"

"Sure"

"Good. I need a break from this crap," I said as I shut down the computer and got up from my desk. "Let's go."

As we walked into my apartment, we could hear the voice of a newscaster.

"All of Manhattan is now under a cloud of smoke and dust. The *city is being evacuated for a two-mile radius around the world Trade Center..."* There was a live shot of the remaining tower and the pile of rubble where the south tower had stood.

Just then, the other tower started to collapse. This time, it seemed that things happened in slow motion. I guess it was just perception. But just like the first tower, the whole thing came straight down. The view was lost by the time it was halfway down though, because of all the dust in the air. Again, in real time, it was over in less than a minute. Another building which took years to construct was gone in the blink of an eye.

"Christ, Fred," was all I could mutter.

We watched for a while then decided to go do something. To be honest, I was having trouble concentrating on anything other than what I had seen on TV. I kept thinking how unlikely it was that one plane could crash into a skyscraper, much less a second one crashing right into the one next door, and yet another into the nerve center of our nation's defenses. It seemed obvious that something more sinister than a computer or radar glitch was at work.

Fred and I decided to split up and check on some of the remodeling jobs which were continuously underway in the apartments. It seemed nobody ever bought a condo and liked it just the way it was. Everybody wanted to customize their new home. Once, an investor dumped nearly half a million dollars into a place and sold it at a profit, only to have the new owner gut it and start over. In fact, I scarfed up the cherry cabinets that the new owner tore out of the kitchen and installed them in my place. Anyway, I thought that checking out the apartments would give me a respite from the disturbing thoughts and images which kept creeping into my brain.

After about an hour or so of visiting with contractors and owners it was apparent that I would not escape the horror. Everyone I met with wanted to discuss the events in New York and Washington. Finally, I called Fred to meet up with me at the office.

"Delaware Two, come in."

"Come back," came Fred's voice.

"Can you meet me on 55 please?"

"10-4, be there in five."

⁓⁓⁓

"Everything's cool in the apartments, except 9104. The guy exposed a bunch of asbestos so I had to shut him down until the abatement contractor takes care of it. Other than that, we're good."

Fred was like a pit bull with the remodelers. If they didn't play by the rules, he'd force them to stop construction.

"Did you hear any more about the Trade Center?" he asked.

"Uh-uh."

"Well, that's all anyone wants to talk about."

"Yeah, I know."

"Did you hear about the other plane that crashed in Pennsylvania?"

"No," I replied. "What's that about?"

"I don't know. I heard it just crashed in a field somewhere."

We chatted for a few more minutes. Then I heard Alan's voice on the radio.

"Delaware One, come in please."

"Come back, Alan," I replied.

"Can you come to 44 please?"

"10-4." Then, to Fred, "Let's go." It was around 11:00 AM.

As we walked toward the elevators I heard the public address system in the stairwells announcing that the commercial portion of the building was being evacuated.

Although the two parts of the building are operated separately, the structure itself was designed as one building and was operated by a single entity when it originally opened. At that time, only the stairwells and commercial areas had an active PA system. By 1973, city ordinances had established more stringent codes for newer buildings. However, buildings like the Hancock were "grandfathered" and not required to comply with the new code. Consequently, no emergency communication system existed in our part of the building, other than the stairwell speakers which were under the control of the commercial operators.

"Man, we better see what's up," I said as we stepped into the elevator. "I don't think we need to worry anymore about the driveway for now, Fred."

"Guess not," he replied.

As we approached the management office, Alan was standing in front of the service desk on the telephone.

"...we'll call you as soon as we know anything. Yes, thank you. Goodbye."

As he hung up, Alan turned to us and said, "I take it you've heard about the other tower and the crash in Pennsylvania. There's no doubt about it now. We're under some sort of attack. Every station is carrying reports. The government has issued a grounding order for all aircraft over the entire country. Did you hear the announcement over the PA?"

"Yeah, the commercial side announced an evacuation order," I said.

"The commercial owners called for an evacuation on their own, but the city has also called for a mandatory evacuation of all Category 1 [over 780' in height] commercial buildings and is strongly recommending a voluntary evacuation of all residential high rises downtown. What do you think we should do?"

"I don't know. We've got a lot of older people who don't have anywhere else to go. Some of them couldn't get out even if they wanted to, without help. I've never had to deal with anything like this before," I stated honestly. "Maybe we should contact Jack and see what he thinks."

"Good idea. Let's go to my office."

Alan dialed Jack Schmidt, who was the board president at that time. "Jack. It's Alan. Are you aware of what's going on? The commercial owners have started evacuating downstairs. The city is calling for a voluntary evacuation of all downtown residential high-rises. Hold on a second, Jack." Alan placed him on hold.

"Harry. Let's get the guys down here so we can get some kind of game plan going."

"Got it," I said.

"This is Delaware One to all Delawares [maintenance personnel]. Please report to the service desk immediately," I said into my walkie-talkie.

Then I turned to Fred. "Confirm with each man that he heard the transmission."

Fred stepped away to call each guy directly as I returned my attention to Alan. He was again speaking to Jack on the phone.

"Harry and the staff will begin a door to door canvass of the apartments, starting at the top, and I'll have the doormen start calling the apartments from the bottom up. Okay? All right, we'll see you then."

As he hung up, we looked at each other as if to say, "What the hell do we do now?"

We walked out to the Sky Lobby to talk when we noticed a mob in front of the elevators. Some people had suitcases, others were carrying their pets. All in all though, everything was orderly. Apparently, the word was already out about the evacuation advisory. This was going to make our job a bit easier.

I noticed one of the residents, Mr. Thomas, waiting for an elevator. He wore a crew cut and for some reason, I started thinking about that Beatles tune. *Here come old flat top, he come groovin' up slowly.*

I returned to the present when I saw some of the shut-ins leaving with their caregivers. Mrs. Adonomos was there, dressed to the nines. Not even an emergency would allow her to be seen in public in less than impeccable attire.

Contractors mingled with the residents. It was getting busy, so Alan called one of the doormen up to 44 to control the number of people who got into an elevator at one time.

About that time, the crew started showing up. Since it was Tuesday, we had a full compliment on the day shift, about eight men altogether. Once everyone was there I began:

"All right, guys. It looks like our country is under some sort of attack. Both of the World Trade Center towers have collapsed. So far it looks like whoever is responsible is targeting skyscrapers and government buildings. We need you to split up and each take a floor starting on 92. Go door to door and knock loudly. If a resident answers, advise them that the city recommends that we evacuate the building. If they refuse, we can't force them. Just write down the apartment number of any resident who tells you they won't be leaving. When you've finished a floor, call the other guys and move to the next floor that hasn't been checked. Got it?"

"10-4, Chief."

"Got it, Harry."

"Wait a minute, guys," Alan said. "Does anyone here feel they have to leave? If you do, it won't be held against you."

Not a man asked to be relieved. I hadn't expected otherwise.

"All right, then. Let's go," I said with a clap of my hands.

As they all took off I turned to Alan. "What do you think of these guys now?"

"Same as I always did. They're the best. Hey, does it seem warm in here to you?"

"Actually, it is kinda muggy. I'm going down to 42 to check things out. I'll get back to you in a bit."

The forty-second floor is a shared mechanical floor. Much of the ventilation equipment for our half of the building is located there, as well as the chillers.

When I exited the elevator I was immediately stunned by the relatively low noise level. It didn't take me long to realize that the chillers had been turned off. Apparently when the commercial owners called for an evacuation, they meant everyone, including their engineering staff. With no one around to monitor their equipment, they had no choice but to shut it down. And since we purchased chilled water from them, we were screwed. It had to be about 80 degrees outside and with 100% outside air being forced into the building; it wouldn't take long to get toasty.

As I walked around to the other side of the machine room floor I noticed all the commercial air handlers were also off. Our fans were still running and I debated whether or not to turn them off. I decided to leave them on for the time being, figuring that some warm air would be better than nothing.

༺༻

"Well, the chillers are down, and nobody's around downstairs," I said to Alan as I walked up to the service desk. "Let me check on the guys and see where we're at with the notification, okay?"

"Good idea," said Alan. "I'll be in the office checking out CNN."

"Delaware Two, come in," I said into my two-way.

"Come back."

"Fred, where are we with the evacuation notice?" I asked.

"Well, a lot of people aren't home," he replied. "Some of the people who were home said they're leaving, but a lot of them said they're not going anywhere. We've been writing down the apartment numbers of the people who said they're staying. We've got about eight more floors to go and we're done. It's getting kinda warm up here, though."

"10-4. At least the apartment A/Cs still work. Carry on and when you're done, get the guys down to 44."

"10-4," was all he said.

༄༄༄

"Do you think we should shut down the ventilation?" Alan asked as we stood around the service desk, watching the diminishing exodus.

"I'm not sure. It's a toss-up. It's about eighty outside now. I don't think it will get any warmer. Do you?"

"No, but somebody on the news, some terrorism expert, was talking about mustard gas and anthrax. He was saying how the government has done studies on how terrorists could use the air intakes to flood a building with the stuff."

"Yeah, but Alan, our lowest intake is 500 feet off the ground. There's no way to get to them from the outside without a rig," I told him.

"What if someone got inside? Could they throw something into the air handlers?" he asked.

"Well, yes. They'd really have to know what they were doing and where to go, though."

"You think that whoever crashed into the Trade Center knew what they were doing and where they were going?" he asked, sarcastically.

"Okay, point taken. I'll shut everything down. I really don't think it will hurt. But the building will go negative compared to the outside. As long as we don't get dusted from the air or something, we'll be all right."

"Right then, let's do it," he said as he walked toward his office. "I'm going to watch the news again for a while. Can you let me know when everything is done?"

"You bet," I said as I headed for the machine rooms.

I contacted Fred and asked him to meet me on the 98th floor so we could start shutting down the fans manually. The guys were finishing up the door to door notification. When Fred arrived, we shut down all the supply fans as well as the exhaust fans. I wanted to keep the building pressure as close to neutral as possible. We systematically checked all the intake dampers to ensure they were completely closed. About fifteen minutes into our routine, my cell phone rang.

"Hello?"

"Harry, you need to get out of there, now." It was Kathy.

"Settle down, Darlin'."

"No, I won't. Why haven't you answered your phone? I've been calling and calling. We watched the towers in New York collapse on TV and the government thinks we're under attack. Even the news people here say that they're evacuating all the tall buildings in Chicago!"

"First of all, you know my phone doesn't work well in the building. And anyway, it's only the commercial and office buildings, hon. We've had a lot of people leave, but a lot decided to stay. We can't bail out now. These people depend on us."

"Bullcrap!" she yelled. "They're not paying you to stay there and die, are they?"

"Nobody's gonna die. None of the guys are sniveling about

leaving. What am I supposed to do, split for home? Oh yeah, that's right, I am home."

"Stop being such a smartass," she snapped. By this time Fred was getting fidgety and trying to act like he wasn't listening.

"Honey, I gotta go now. I'll call you later, all right?"

"Fine. But if you wind up dead, it's your own damn fault."

"Yes, Darlin'. I promise I won't blame you if I die." Fred was now looking down and kind of grinning. "I love you and I'll call you later, all right?"

"Well, you better, big shot. I love you. Bye."

Fred and I carried on with securing the ventilation on 98. When we were finished, we headed for 42.

"You need to call your wife, or something?" I asked Fred while we were securing S-16.

"Nah, I called her earlier. They sent everybody home a while ago."

Fred's wife was a librarian at the Washington Library, which was technically a civil service position. Apparently, City Hall wouldn't waste an opportunity to take the day off with pay.

"I guess Kathy's pushin' hard for you to leave, huh?"

"Yeah, but it's not gonna happen. What am I gonna do, move in with you?" I asked. "You never even have any decent beer, butthead!"

We laughed and continued talking about the towers and the devastation we had seen on TV. I guess it hadn't really sunk in yet. It was still kind of like watching the replay of a train wreck; sort of far away and surreal.

We continued shutting down the fans. When we were done, the total silence on the floor was creepy. Now that all the machinery was off, I could actually "feel" the quiet. When we were finished, we took the stairs up to 44 to see what else was going on. It was about 12:15 PM

It was kind of eerie, walking past our grocery store in the middle of the day and seeing the closed sign on the door and the lights out.

As we approached the service desk, Alan came out of the office and said, "Well, they've grounded nearly all the planes now. Only a couple left in the air and they're being escorted by fighter jets to the nearest airport."

By now, most of the residents who intended to leave had already done so. We stood around the service desk and conversed for awhile, waiting for the rest of the crew to show up.

When everybody arrived I said to Alan, "How about we send a couple guys down to Johnny Rocket's for some grease burgers or something? The store is closed, so we can't even get anything to drink."

"Good idea. Let me get the office credit card. Lunch is on the Association today."

While Alan was digging around for the credit card, I told the apprentice, Jake, to start making a list of what everybody wanted. I wanted a cheese burger deluxe, which came with a fried egg on it, the way they made burgers in Wales when I was stationed there in the Navy.

After Jake got everyone's order, I said, "Take Clemente with you and go get the food. And don't screw around down there either, I'm not kiddin'."

While we were all waiting around I got a call from the Curtis, the doorman.

"Delaware One, come in please."

"Come back."

"Harry, can you call me on the telephone, please?"

"10-4."

I called the door station from the service desk. "What's up, Curtis?"

"I know you don't like me talkin' about this stuff on the radio. It's Mrs. Newton. She says she gots to leave but Ulysses got hisself in trouble and she can't get him into his cage."

Great. Mr. Stupid got himself in trouble once again, did he? I could only imagine. This was just what I needed today.

"Hey, Harry?"

"Yeah?"

"She also says the power is out in her apartment."

"All right already," I said and hung up.

Here we go again, I thought.

"I'm going to 5620," I said to nobody in particular and headed for the low rise.

When I knocked at her door, Mrs. Newton answered in her usual frantic tone.

"Oh hurry, Harry. Ulysses has gotten himself all tangled up in some strings or wires or something under the sofa!"

As I walked in, I noticed that she had her hand wrapped in a towel.

"What happed to your hand, Mrs. Newton?" I asked.

"Well when I found Ulysses under the sofa all tangled up, I tried to get him out and I couldn't because everything was knotted up and so I got some scissors and started cutting. Suddenly there was a big bunch of sparks and my hand got burned. And Ulysses must have gotten frightened because he started writhing around and got himself tangled up even worse."

It didn't take a brain surgeon to figure this one out.

"So the power is out as well?" I asked.

"Yes, that's right. I think I must have cut a wire or something."

You think?!

"Well, let's see what we can do about Ulysses first, then we'll see about the power," I said. I must confess, I had thought about resetting the breakers first, just to see what would happen.

"So where's he at?"

"Oh, he's under the sofa in the den," she stated. "But I think he's in a bad mood."

I'll just bet he is, I thought. "Let's take a look."

I walked into the den and over to the sofa. It was one of those with a skirt around the bottom so you couldn't see all the dust bunnies underneath. I got down on my hands and knees, lifted the skirt, and took a gander.

Sure enough, just as I suspected there was a rat's nest of phone wires and lamp cords, in the middle of which was ensnared my arch nemesis, Ulysses. He was looking even more evil than usual.

"Got yourself in a pickle, eh dumbass?" I whispered.

I could understand the idiot cat getting himself hogtied, but for the life of me, I couldn't figure out how an educated woman could not know the difference between wires and strings! And there, lying next to the jumble of wires was a set of pinking shears with a notch burnt through both blades.

Now, I had seen this sort of thing before. Just about every mechanical tradesman has at least one set of wire pliers with a similar defect lying in his tool box. It's what you get when you cut through both the neutral and hot wire simultaneously, creating a dead short. Only, wire pliers are insulated, so you just end up with a ruined tool, a blown fuse, and spots before your eyes for a while. In this case, Mrs. Newton ended up with a second degree burn.

"Mrs. Newton, do you realize that the mess under here is not strings? It's all extension cords and phone lines."

"Of course I know that NOW," she said with an edge. "At the moment, I'm more concerned with rescuing Ulysses, if you don't mind."

"Alrighty, then," I muttered.

After unplugging all the extension cords in the room, I then made my first attempt at freeing Mr. Ulysses. He wasn't going for it. As soon as I got close, he started hissing and twisting around, getting even more entangled.

Now, I like to think I'm the kind of man who learns from his mistakes, eventually. Boomer put the hurt on me real good when I messed with him. I had no intention of getting sliced and diced by another mangy feline.

"He's pretty riled up, Mrs. Newton." I said. "Maybe we should let him be for a while."

"We don't have a while. Terrorists are trying to blow us all up and we need to get out of here now!" she said, her voice rising.

"But, Mrs. Newton..."

"Just get him out so we can leave!" she practically screamed.

"All right, all right. But, I'm not going under this sofa again. Let's lift it and move it over so we can see a bit better."

I knew I was asking a lot, since she only weighed about ninety pounds, but there was no way I was going to risk getting torn to shreds by Ulysses. If I could stand up while I worked, I'd have a better chance of avoiding his claws. Unlike Boomer, I knew from experience that all of Ulysses' defenses were in excellent working order.

"Fine," she said with an air of contempt. She took one end and I took the other.

"On the count of three," I directed her. "One, two, three," and together we lifted the sofa and took two steps to the left (my left, that is). Then we set it down.

There was Prince Ulysses! All trussed up like a beef roast. You're not so clever now, are you? I mused.

"It should be fairly easy to get him out now, Mrs. Newton," I said as I walked over to him. But as soon as I got near, he started rolling around, hissing and kicking.

"Maybe you should try to get him loose," I said to her.

"Well, I never!" she said with disdain as she reached down to free him.

He didn't settle down right away, though. I guess he was still blinded by the flash when she snipped through the lamp cord.

Then came the singing. "Ulyyyysses. You're such a pretty boyoy. Mama's pretty boyoy."

As bad as I thought her voice sucked, it started working (like always) and he began to settle down. He allowed her to start untangling the wires, so I figured it was safe for me to give her a hand. Bad move! The second I touched one of the wires, he clawed at me with his back leg. He missed, but that was all it took for me to get the message.

"I guess Ulysses doesn't want my help today."

"Yes, I can see that," she said without sympathy and resumed her singing.

"What a beautiful boyoy."

Before long, she had the little bastard free and asked me to get his travel cage. Man, that thing was like an Airstream camper! The inside was padded and covered in velvet. It probably had TV, too.

As she put him in, I saw him looking at me as if to say, "Catch ya lata, sucka!"

"We're leaving soon. Now, would you mind having a look at the power before you go, please?" she asked with disdain.

"Of course, Mrs. Newton," I replied as I walked to the breaker box. I opened the door and checked all the breakers. As I suspected, none were tripped, which meant she most likely blew a main line fuse back at the meter vault.

"Well, it looks like the main is blown. I'll go check it out and I'll be right back," I said as I walked to the door.

"Please don't take too long," she called after me as I left the apartment.

The vault was one floor up, so I took the stairs. I entered and located her meter; I opened the main breaker, and sure enough, one of the huge fuses was smoked. I had to go to the store room on 48 and rummage around until I located the proper fuse. Then I had to get some tools from the shop since fuses of that size were bolted in.

In about twenty minutes I had replaced the bad fuse and closed the breaker. The meter immediately began to spin. So far, so good.

I returned to the apartment and found the door locked, so I knocked. After about a minute, I knocked again.

This time, without opening the door, she called out "It's back on now. Thank you," and once again, that was it. I was dismissed without as much as a dollar bill.

"Okay, bye." Then to myself, "You're welcome, Granny Tight-ass! I hope your cab breaks down on Lake Shore Drive…in the middle of rush-hour…in a thunderstorm!"

When I arrived back at the party room, everybody was wolfing down burgers and fries.

"Hey, chief. Over here. I saved your burger from Fred," called Clemente.

"Thanks, Clemente. You got something to drink with that?" I asked as I walked over and sat down.

"Sure, chief. Got some soda right here."

I was facing east, looking out over the lake. It didn't take long for me to notice another first time occurrence; there were no planes in the sky, out over the water.

Nearly all large aircraft headed for O'Hare are directed out over Lake Michigan. Normally, at any time of day, you'd see at least half a dozen planes circling or lining up for the approach. Regardless of where they come from, they all seem to fly in from the east and follow the Kennedy all the way to the airport. But now, the skies were empty.

"You guys notice the lack of airplanes out there?" I asked.

"Yeah, we were just talking about it," said Ronnie. "I don't ever remember there being like, no planes."

"What do they do during the air show?" asked Jake.

"I don't know. I guess they reroute them or something," I said. "You can't have F-18s and Stealth Bombers doing rolls in front of airliners."

"Yeah, the F-18s and Stealth Bombers will be busy as soon as we find out who did the Trade Center and the Pentagon."

I don't recall who said that, but we all got kinda quiet for a couple of minutes. I dug into my cheeseburger and cold fries. Someone asked me how things went with Ulysses. I mumbled something like "awesome" without enthusiasm. Normally, we would have all had a good laugh over my tale, but I just didn't feel like telling it at the time.

Right about then, Alan walked in and stated, "The commercial side just shut down the garage. The only people left on their side of the building are some security guards. If you leave the garage, you'll need your monthly pass and a picture ID, and you must submit to a vehicle search to get your vehicle back in -- even you, Harry."

What a clusterf--k! I thought.

"Does everybody understand?" Alan asked. "They've already secured the dock and turned away some of our vendors and contractors."

Everyone started talking at once until a voice came over our radios.

"Apartment maintenance -- come in, please."

"Come back," I replied with a mouth full of cold cheeseburger. It wasn't like anyone else was going to answer.

"This is Captain Swain. Can you call me at control on a land line right away, sir?" The commercial security force was nothing if not polite.

"10-4."

I dumped what was left of my lunch in the trash can and walked over to the house phone on the wall.

"Hey. This is Harry," I said into the phone when security answered.

"Hi, Harry. This is Swain. Looks like we've got a code two, again. Nothing specific. Can you and your guys check out the stairwells and that?"

"Yeah, sure. What's a code two again?" I'm such a dumbass.

"Bomb threat," Swain laughed into the phone.

I should have known. It's not like we hadn't gotten bomb threats before. They always turned out to be bogus. But this particular day, we had to take it a lot more seriously.

"Oh, yeah. You know that we wouldn't know a bomb from a micro-wave, right?"

Swain chuckled. "Neither would we! But we gotta try, don't we?"

"Yeah. We'll call you if we find anything."

"We'll do the same. Remember though, radio silence, all right?"

"Sure. Later."

Great! This really sucked. We wouldn't even be able to communicate unless we were face to face. I walked back to the tables and said, "Code two, boys. We need to get busy." Nobody even asked what a code two was.

"Do you guys even know what a code two is?" I asked as everybody started throwing away their garbage.

"Bomb threat," they all called out in unison. It seemed I was the only moron who couldn't remember my codes.

"All right, let's check the stairwells, the corridors and the chute rooms. Fred and I will check the machinery rooms. If anybody finds anything suspicious, you know what to do"

"10-4, Chief!"

"You got it."

"We don't touch anything, and we report back to you."

"No radios, guys," I reaffirmed. The fear had always been that a radio transmission could trigger a bomb. "Let's go!"

Fred and I headed for 42 first. The rest of the guys went to the stairwells and the corridors. After about an hour, we had all returned to the 44th floor, so I called Swain.

"Hey Swain, it's Harry. We're cool up here. How about you guys?"

"Yeah. We got nothin'."

"Kinda quiet down there, I bet," I said.

"Yeah, it's like a graveyard," Swain replied.

"Well, good luck. We'll keep in touch."

"Thanks, Harry. See ya 'round." And he hung up.

For the rest of the afternoon we all tried to carry on with our normal duties. To be honest, there wasn't much to do, what with everyone gone and the dock closed. At 4:00 PM, the evening shift showed up. Everyone was there in the maintenance office. We all started to swap information when once again, like clockwork, my cell phone rang.

"Hello."

"Harry, you have to get out of that building!" It was Kathy. She sounded pretty whipped up.

"It's all right now, honey. Everything has calmed down now."

"No it hasn't. You're just saying that. You don't know what's going on, nobody does!" Her voice was starting to crack a bit.

"Look Darlin'. It's shift change time and I've got things to go over with the guys. Let me call you back on a land line in a couple of minutes, okay?"

"No! I want you to promise me you're going to leave and come out to my house right now!" She was starting to cry.

"C'mon, hon. You know I can't leave right now. I'll call you back in a few minutes." Everybody in the office got quiet.

"You're such a jerk! The news even said that all the well-known skyscrapers are high risk and you just want to be a tough guy, like always."

"Kathy, settle down. Everything is fine. All the planes are grounded now and the government is on top of it. I'll call you back in a bit, all right?"

"Harry, I'm really scared. Please come out to the house." She was practically begging. But I couldn't leave. And I truly believed we were in no danger.

"Hon, I'll call you back — I love you and I won't let you down, but I gotta go." I told her I loved her one more time and hung up.

"What the hell are you all lookin' at?" I snapped at the guys as I put my phone in my pocket.

Nobody said anything. I finished briefing the evening shift on what to do, and then headed up to my apartment. When I arrived I immediately called Kathy. She was just this side of hysterical. The fact that the news coverage alternated between an endless video loop of the destruction and government officials double-talking didn't help. But in the end, I promised her that if anything bad happened in Chicago, I would leave and head to her house, and I meant it.

The rest of the evening was pretty much the same as it was all day. Every network carried the same coverage and speculation about who was responsible. The skies over the city were empty and quiet, with the exception of the fighter jets which had begun patrolling around downtown.

I finally decided to watch a sci-fi movie and try to stop thinking about what would happen tomorrow. Tomorrow would be here soon enough. Around 10:00 PM I called Kathy again to say good night, and went to bed.

I found it peculiar, lying there looking out the window at the darkness. Unexpectedly, I realized that I missed the parade of blinking aircraft lights, which normally proceeded northwest across the sky toward O'Hare. Until that day, I guess we all took "normal" for granted. I had no idea, as I drifted off to sleep, how much life was about to change, especially for those of us who lived in the clouds.

Wednesday morning started a lot different from all the days before. After my morning dose of bad news on the Today show and my customary conversation with Kathy, I headed down stairs. The normal morning rush of residents heading to work could best be described as a weak trickle. So many people had left the building that it seemed like a ghost town. The market on 44 remained closed.

The overnight reports from the midnight shift and the afternoon shift from the previous day were as to be expected, given the circumstances; more bomb threats, complaints about the corridor temperature, and frantic phone calls from out of town residents.

The huge dumpster at the dock was full and no trash could be moved until it was emptied. Unfortunately, the dock remained closed to all traffic so we could not get a pick up. I ordered the compactors shut down and the trash chute doors locked.

I had some coffee and instructed the crew to go about their business the way they always did. I then headed to the management office to discuss the game plan with Alan.

"Morning. Looks like we're in a bit of a jam today," I said as I walked into Alan's office and proceeded to inform him of the trash situation.

"Just one more hassle we can add to the growing list. I'll have to put out a notice to the residents anyway, so I'll add a blurb about the trash. What else?"

"Well, I think we should get all the ventilation equipment back on line. Have you heard from commercial?" I asked.

"Yeah. The building is still closed but their engineering and security staff is back on site. They've increased security by like, 300%. The garage is also still closed. Oh, and it looks like your driveway project is on hold."

"What's up with that?"

"We're discussing plans to install barriers around the building to prevent any vehicles from getting close enough to cause damage, which means the drive way will be closed indefinitely," he replied. "We and the Sears are considered high risk targets. The Sears is still closed completely. It sounds like the government is pretty much convinced that the whole Trade Center attack as well as the other stuff, was planned by that Osama bin Laden nut-ball. The cops have been ordered to tow any vehicle left unattended, anywhere near us."

I'd never even heard of 'Sama bin Laden. "Right, then. We'll get going on the ventilation. Hopefully, they have a chiller back up. I'll check with you later, all right?"

"Yeah, sounds good," he said. And as I left he added, "Have a nice day!"

⁓⁓⁓

We spent the morning starting up the fans, setting temperatures, and talking about what was going on. I convinced the commercial engineers to give us some chilled water. The place was kind of quiet. Not many work orders or emergencies.

I heard from Kathy every now and then. Every once in a while I would sneak home and catch a few minutes of CNN.

By Thursday evening, there were contractors dropping Jersey rails around the building. You know, those interlocking concrete barriers used in construction zones. I had to have a couple of them reset to allow residents being dropped off to walk up to the entrance from the street.

The place resembled a fortress by Friday morning. The garage remained closed for over a month. The revenue lost by the commercial owners was more than I earned in a year.

Only residents and employees were allowed into the garage (as Alan had earlier informed us) and we had to submit to a thorough search and show picture IDs and valid parking passes. When Kathy came up for the weekend I had a hell of a time finding a place to park her car. Street parking in downtown Chicago? Forget about it. All the other local garages were double parking to take up the slack, so I finally found a spot. On Christmas Day 2001, Kathy had to unwrap the presents she brought me at the newly erected guard shack, even though by that time the guards all knew her. To say the least, things were really starting to suck around Big John.

It was over a week before planes were seen in the air again. But none were seen over the city for quite some time, unless you counted fighter jets on patrol. The FAA had established a no-fly zone over the downtown area which lasted for months.

The Association and the commercial owners agreed, on the advice of the government and the insurance companies, that the plaza should be reconfigured to permanently protect the building from any form of ground-based assault (car bombs in particular). So a new design incorporating more granite clad planters as well as steel bollards encased in granite was presented by Skidmore, Owings & Merrill. Construction began in the spring of '02. Access to the building during that period was a huge pain in the ass. Many other buildings downtown followed suit.

Of course, security within the building became equally unpleasant. Residents were eventually required to use electronic card keys multiple times to go anywhere within the building. If you ordered a pizza, you had to go down to the front desk to pick it up. I must confess, moving out to the country and pumping gas for a living was starting to appeal to me.

Sometimes the little things have the potential for becoming the most aggravating. I recall when, after many months, both entities (home owners and commercial owners) agreed upon a security protocol, whereby every employee, commercial or residential, as well as residents, would be required to obtain a card key from both sides in order to pass from one portion of the building to the other.

Every person that lived or worked in the condominium section had to go to the commercial management office to submit a written request for a card key bearing their picture. Of course, the commercial building employees would have to receive a similar access card from us. This protocol was much more aggravating to the residents than to anyone else, since this was their home rather than their work place.

The day I went to the commercial management office to pick up my ID/access card key, there was a new receptionist of about twenty-two years of age. She was kind of cute and seemed friendly, so I struck up a conversation.

"Hello. You're new here, aren't you?"

"Yes, I am. My name is Ellen. Who are you?" she asked.

"I'm Harry Budge, the chief engineer from upstairs," I stated, casually. "How long have you been here?"

"Since last week. I just started with the company. Today is my first full day."

"Well," I said, "I need a card key. I was told that you needed a picture."

"Yes. I can take one of you now. Then it will take about ten minutes to encode the card and apply the photo. No big deal," she said with a smile.

"So how do you like it so far?" I asked.

"Great," she said enthusiastically.

"Yeah, but all this security is a real drag, isn't it?" That's when I got aggravated.

"Well, that's just the world we live in," she stated matter-of-factly.

Now I don't know for sure what ticked me off about that. Whether it was the fact that she was only a kid that had started like, yesterday, or that condescending tone or that she so easily accepted the way our lives were changing or that she hadn't a clue what it felt like to have to use a card key just to move around in a building you called home.

I was tempted to start lecturing her about what it meant to live in America, but I resisted the urge. What could I say? Instead, I mumbled something meaningless, stood against the wall while she took my picture, and then sat down to wait for my new card key.

While I waited, I thought about Orwell's book *1984*. Big Brother, etc. When she returned with my new security card, I had a whole new reason to be pissed off.

"What does the big T stand for?" I asked.

"It means tenant," she stated innocently.

"I'm not a tenant. I'm a resident and an employee of 175 E. Delaware Place," I said with indignation.

"Yes, I understand," she said. "But we only have three categories in our system: Employee, Contractor, and Tenant."

"But the residents are not your tenants. They own the top half of the building." I was getting territorial, I guess.

"I'm sorry Mr. Budge. That's just the way it is. I can't change it. It's just the world we live in."

There. She said it again, with that same tone in her voice. I wanted to rip her face off, but all I said was "Well, I'll see ya 'round," and I left. But I silently vowed to make sure that when she came to 44 for her ID/access card, it would be emblazoned with a capital "B" for -- well, use your imagination!

It didn't take long for the government to identify who was responsible for 9/11. After that, things got kinda dicey around the city.

Anybody that appeared to be of Middle Eastern descent was looked at with suspicion. Cabbies and convenience store owners were getting the crap kicked out of them left and right.

Luke and Matt started talking about dropping out of college to join the military, which didn't bode well with Kathy.

"Well, Harry joined the Navy when he was only seventeen," I remember Luke saying to his mom.

"Yes. He was also a dropout, burnout bum, which is why he had to enlist in the first place," she replied. "No offense, Harry."

Ouch! "Uh, no problem."

Okay. So I'd been involved in some "incidents" when I was a teenager and a stint in the Navy was a recommendation from a juvie judge. But in my own defense, I earned my GED while in the Navy and finished my education on the GI bill after I was discharged. But that's another story.

Within six or seven months, the hard rain began to fall on Afghanistan. I recall watching the news clips of the fleet heading out to sea. Ships of all shapes and sizes: destroyers, cruisers, troop transports, tenders and support vessels, and of course, aircraft carriers. Soon, I caught myself singing, "Here come old flat top, he come groovin' up slowly." But I started changing the words around. "He got cruisin' missiles ...he got lots of napalm."

At first, I thought it was really funny and I actually spent time changing up the whole song. "Come and get some, right now, a piece of me!" I even taught the crew my new version of the classic during morning coffee. I guess it was my way of dealing with the rage I felt, and the helplessness that accompanied it.

I was actually ecstatic when the first wave of bombers dropped their payloads. After all, those bastards deserved it, right? But they weren't the only ones that got a taste.

In March, 2003, President Bush introduced the Iraqis to "Shock and Awe." As I slowly began to realize how apathetic I was becoming to the death and destruction I watched each night on the TV, I recalled another war.

I remembered protesting that war as a freshman high school student, proclaiming outrage at the nightly body counts and photos of maimed children and dead civilians. I remembered the trial of Lt. Calley and his men. And, I remembered the words and actions of the Beatles and John Lennon in particular.

Lennon's songs were his way of trying to get people to stop the killing and "give peace a chance." But, there I was; hating and wanting blood -- anybody's blood, and distorting his songs to vocalize my hate.

As I considered my dilemma, shame and sadness gradually replaced my rage and hate. I recalled the words to one of John Lennon's greatest songs; *Imagine*. Of course, I knew then, just as I had come to realize when I enlisted in the Navy during the final days of that other war that the people of the world weren't ready to "live as one." Recalling the videos of women and children dancing in the streets of Saudi Arabia and other middle-eastern countries on September 12th 2001, I realized that they probably wouldn't be ready in my lifetime.

I was having trouble getting my head around the idea, that life was different now. I guess I just wanted things to be the way they were. Before 9/11, I mean. I decided I didn't care for the world we were now destined to live in.

But one day, I awoke, thinking of yet another Beatles tune, one that soon became my mantra. I began to play it every morning while I showered, and I sang it to myself throughout the day.

Even now, years later, when I find myself waiting in line at an airport security check point, jonesing for the old days, I can feel the galloping drum beat start to build in my head, like a rider-less horse, bearing down from a distance. Then, as TSA personnel rifle through my carry-on bag, I'll begin to hum the mellow, blues-y guitar riffs. And if you happen to be standing near me in that security line, while I'm re-packing my stuff and re-donning my shoes, you just might want to join me when I start singing: *"Get back ...Get back ...Get back to where you once belonged."* What? It could happen. Yeah, if only. Right?

The Alejandro Affair

"This show is dreadful," Kathy whispered to me. We were at the Drury Lane Theater in the Water Tower Mall across the street.

"Actually, I was gonna say it sucks!" I said. "You wanna leave at intermission and go get a drink at the Saloon?"

We loved the theater, particularly musicals. But, we were discriminating. Since we belonged to a theater club called "Broadway in Chicago," we had reserved seats at all the big theaters for every show in the season. Of course, we had to accept that some performances would be duds, but it was worth it to have good seats for the blockbusters. We didn't mind much if the occasional stinker sneaked its way into the rotation. At least we didn't need a cab to get home this time.

"Yeah, this is starting to hurt."

We endured the rest of the first half of the show as a courtesy. We even applauded, out of sympathy, when the curtain fell.

In addition to the discomfort of watching the hacks make a train wreck of what should have been a good show, I was developing a headache. I was wearing my new, awesomely cool, progressive lens wonder glasses, but I couldn't really focus on anything. I felt like an idiot, nodding to someone speaking a foreign language. No matter what was going on, I couldn't seem to find the sweet spot where everything was clear. But man, was I lookin' good! Anyway, we abandoned our seats and left the theater.

It was a warm summer night and the walk to the Saloon was pleasant. We had a martini, discussed the crappy show, and decided to go home and order in. Curtis, the doorman, said hello and opened the door. As we entered the lobby, I noticed a tall guy with dark hair near the entrance with a tripod setup, taking photos of the lobby.

Now, this was odd for several reasons. First, it was late in the evening and the management office was closed. Second, I had no knowledge that photos were going to be taken anywhere in the building that day, and since I was in charge of security in our part of the building during off hours, I should have been informed. Since 9/11, the residents were particularly touchy about people taking photos around the property, for obvious reasons.

To begin with, the Association charged a fee for that privilege. Several movies had been shot on site previously, most notably one of the *Poltergeist* movies as well *Stranger than Fiction* (the Association always made out like bandits). Secondly, the guy looked to be of middle-eastern descent (uh-oh). Since September eleventh, that fact alone was cause for suspicion in the eyes of most people.

I went directly to the desk where Jimmy, the desk man, was intent on watching a pocket television, instead of watching what was going on in the lobby or what was happening on the security monitors. Kathy just sort of hung around, admiring the painting which was hung near the seating area. She got bored in a hurry when I was dispensing my duties.

I asked, "So, who's the dude taking pictures?"

Jimmy looked up and said, while turning off the TV, "Uh, I don't know his name, but, uh, he's a real estate agent and I've seen him in here before."

"Oh. I get it. Since he's a real estate agent whom you've seen here before, you don't have to know his name or have him sign in or anything, right?"

"Um, uh..."

"Does he have written permission to be taking pictures?"

He looked at me with that "deer in the headlights" look and said, "Um, I'm not sure, uh..."

"What do you mean, you're not sure? It's your job to monitor what's going on around here, Jimmy."

He started to mutter something, but I really wasn't interested in his bullshit. Based on my experience, I figured the guy probably greased his palm to look the other way.

It is a universal truth that doormen can be bought. Five bucks gets you twenty minutes in the NO PARKING zone, twenty gets your mistress in the building while the wife is away, no questions asked. Anyway, I turned away and walked over to the guy with the camera.

"Excuse me sir, do you have written permission to be photographing the property?" I asked when I was about three feet away.

The guy looked up from his camera, without lifting his head and said, "Who the f--k are you?"

Now I don't know about everywhere else, but in *Back of the Yards*, (where I was raised) you didn't speak to anybody that way, unless you wanted a fat lip. And when it comes to the operation of the building, particularly with regard to security, nobody challenged my authority.

Needless to say, I was hot. So, I said, "Let's see. I'm the f--ker in charge of f--kin' security for this f--kin' property. . . F--kface! So I'm asking you again, do you have written permission to take photos of our lobby or not?"

That got his attention. He straightened up and gave me the once-over. He was about an inch or two taller than me and a few years younger. I guess that's what prompted him to press his luck. "Who says I need permission to take pictures -- you?" he said with a belligerent tone.

So then I took a step forward, got in his face and said, "Yeah, that's right, me."

I could see he was thinking again at that point. Then he looked away while packing up his gear and said, "No matter, I got what I need. Who are you anyway, the janitor?"

If we had been outside, I'd have knocked him on his butt. But instead, I said, "Nah, I'm just a guy who doesn't care for sleazy real estate agents taking pictures in his lobby." I could exchange insults with the best of them. "So if you don't leave the property now, I'll have you escorted out by security officers," I added.

So he comes back with, "One phone call, and I could have your job." If I only had a nickel for every time I heard that one.

"Yeah, whatever, start calling on your way out."

He continued packing up his stuff, so I started to walk away. But, right on cue, just like a snot-nosed punk, he started with his mouth again. "You're nothing but a glorified janitor; I could have you fired by tomorrow."

So of course, I had to respond in kind. "What do you do for a real job, jerk-off; suck farts outta seat cushions at the Greyhound station?" I loved that one. I got it from a hillbilly I worked with at the power plant at Electro-Motive Division, some years earlier.

By that time, I noticed Kathy had left the lobby, presumably to go to the apartment. She never hung around when I got into altercations. Women don't mind so much if you're fighting over/for them, but they seem to have little tolerance if you get into it with someone over anything else. Just as well, I thought.

So then, the jerk said, "You'll be sorry tomorrow when I get you fired."

"You'll be sorry now if you don't get your ass out of this lobby," I shot back.

The insults continued back and forth; each time he took a step toward the door, he'd say something smart-assed. Then, I would take a step toward him, like herding a cow, and say something back.

Just as he was going through the revolving door he said, "You'll be lucky to be working in the projects, cleaning up dog shit when I'm finished with you." Then he was outside.

I followed him out and said to Curtis, who was gazing up at the sky, looking for UFOs presumably, since stars were nearly impossible to see downtown, due to the light pollution, "If this guy tries to enter the property again, I want you to call the cops, got it?"

That's when I knew just who had duked whom. I saw Curtis glance over at Mr. Dickweed, who looked back, kinda smug like. So I said again, "You got it, Curtis?"

"Uh, yeah, Harry, I got it," he said as he resumed his sky watch.

"You really suck," I heard this guy say behind my back as I turned to re-enter the lobby. I decided to let that one slide and go home since it was obvious that I had established who was in charge. Alas, it was not to be. The jerk just couldn't accept defeat.

"See. That's why I don't respect you. I can say anything I want and you won't do anything about it."

Any dumbass could have seen that for exactly what it was. He knew he was beaten so he figured if he could provoke me into slugging him, he could nail me for assault or something. Well, maybe it was the martini, or maybe I just had enough of this guy's mouth, but instead of walking back into the lobby and letting it go like the smart guy I am, I took the bait.

"What did you say?" I asked as I walked over to him.

"You heard me."

"Say it again and see what happens," I dared him.

"I said 'you suck and I can say anything I want and you won't do anything about it--cuz you're a pussy'."

"Is that right?" I asked as I stepped right up into his face. Before he finished nodding I said, "Suck on this, Sally," and threw a right at his jaw. Now it may have been the alcohol or possibly my funky new tri-focals or even a combination of both. Whatever, my aim was off and I barely scraped his chin. Regardless, he made a big production out of falling on the ground, with his camera crap rolling in every direction.

But, in a flash, he jumped back up as if he had springs up his ass and landed on his feet with a cell phone in his hand. "I got you now, you bastard. I'm calling the cops."

Then he shouted over to Curtis, "Did you see that? He hit me." Curtis just ignored him. I think he knew which side his bread was really buttered on.

"I don't care who you call, bitch, but if you set foot in this lobby again, you'll need that phone to call an ambulance." With that, I went back into the lobby, leaving butt face dialing madly on his phone.

I had no sooner entered the apartment when the house phone rang.

"Hello."

"Yeah, Harry?" It was Jimmy. "The police are down here."

"All right, Jimmy," and I hung up.

"Looks like I've gotta go back down to the lobby, Darlin'. The cops are here," I said to Kathy, who was just gearing up for her twenty questions routine.

"Why?" she asked, with squinty eyes and an accusatory tone. "What's going on? What did you do?"

"Nothing -- I'll tell you later," I said as I walked out the door. I hadn't the time or desire to listen to her lecture me right then.

When I walked into the lobby, Dickweed was near the desk, talking to one of the cops, a short red haired guy. He was all animated, giving the cop his version of how I brutally attacked him, I figured.

The other cop, who was about my height, was talking to Curtis near the front entrance. When they saw me coming, the dude pointed and said, "That's him, Officer, the guy with the beard and the ponytail!"

So I point at my chest and say, "Who, me?"

The short cop told the guy to go sit down, and came up and said to me in an Irish brogue, "This gentleman claims ya assaulted him."

"Well, Officer, I don't think you got the whole story," I stated calmly.

"Yeah? So what's yur story? And I'm tellin' ya right now, if I tink yur bullshittin' me, I'm gonna drag ya in, get it?" Great, I thought. I hope this guy's not the "good cop."

"Okay, here's the deal. I'm the chief engineer of this property and I confronted this guy when I came home and saw him photographing the lobby. He started getting all sassy, and insulting me. So I told him that if he didn't leave, I would have him escorted out and…"

"I don't care about any o' dat. I want to know why ya assaulted him," the cop interrupted.

"I didn't assault anybody." I said. "When we got outside, he wouldn't shut up and kept provoking me. When he called me a pussy, I swung at him, I admit it. But I never even touched him."

"What makes ya tink ya have da right to swing at him because he insulted ya? According to him, ya belted him in da face."

So I look over at Dickweed, and he's just smirking like Sylvester the Cat after swallowing Tweety Pie.

I turned back to the cop and said, "I just told you I never touched him. Check him out. He doesn't have a scratch on him!"

Right about then, the other cop walks up and says, "The doorman says he didn't see anything, Flynn."

Way to go, Curtis, I thought.

"No surprise there," the tall cop continued. "These guys work together, you know. Why don't you let me talk to this guy and you talk to the other doorman, all right?" Flynn didn't seem to like that much, but he grunted and complied.

"You know, my partner," the tall cop says to me, "is kind of a hard ass. He wants to take you in. So just tell me what happened and I'll see if we can sort this out without anybody going to jail." Ah, I thought. This must be the "Good Cop."

So I gave him my version. I explained to him my duty to the property and how since 9/11, we were even more diligent. I gave him the same story I told the other cop about the actual "assault." He seemed a bit more sympathetic to my side of the story.

"Look," he said. "This guy wants to file charges against you. Lucky for you, there's no witnesses. But my partner wants somebody's head. Now, I'm not telling you your business, but it seems to me like you've got a trespassing situation here." Looking at me with raised eyebrows, he left it at that. Say no more! I thought. I get the picture.

The short cop walked back over to us and said, "I'm tinkin' we gotta haul dis fella in, Bill," as he scowled at me.

That's when I went into my spiel. "That's all right, officer. But you're going to have to take him in too," I said while I pointed my thumb toward Dickweed. "I'm filing charges on behalf of the property against this guy for trespassing. He doesn't live or work here, and I asked him to leave politely. He refused, which led to the rest of the incident."

Flynn got pissed when I said that. He looked at the other cop, who simply shrugged.

Then it was the other guy's turn in the barrel with him. He looked across the lobby and says, "Yur card says 175 E. Delaware Place. What's da story?" Apparently, Flynn was bent on getting a piece of somebody's ass.

The guy said, "I use this as my business address."

"Wait a minute," I interjected. "This is a residential property. By code, no businesses are allowed. And I'm telling you, this guy doesn't live here."

"Shut up!" Flynn yelled at me. "I'm talkin' ta him," he growled as he pointed at Dickweed. "And what da hell's wrong witch ya, anyway?"

"What?"

"Why the hell are ya noddin' yur head like an idjit?" I must have been doing my bobbing-for-apples routine, trying to focus.

"Sorry, it's my new glasses," I said, and consciously forced myself to stop nodding.

"Well, cut it out. I'm gettin' seasick just watchin' ya. And keep yur trap shut!"

"Now wait a minute, Flynn," said Bill. "He's right. What gives?"

They both look over at the guy with suspicion. I think Flynn was refocusing his wrath by then. It was starting to look like Dickweed was making an ass out him.

So he said, "You, get yur ass over here," as he waved the guy over. "Yur card says **Alejandro Mendez, Luxury Properties, 175 E. Delaware Place**. Ya don't live here and ya don't work here, so why are ya usin' dis address?"

I couldn't resist. "See, that's what I'm talkin' about."

"I told ya to shut yur pie hole," Flynn snapped.

Bill gave me a look as if to say, "You're winning here, just let it be." So I did what Flynn said and zipped it.

"Well, I show a lot of properties here and..."

"That ain't what I asked ya. Why are ya usin' dis address if ya don't live here or have an office here?"

After about two minutes of this Alejandro guy trying to bullshit his way out of it and Flynn getting more pissed by the second, I knew I had the upper hand. Finally, Bill piped up.

"Well Flynn, what do you wanna do? It looks to me like we either take 'em both in or neither of 'em. This guy says he was assaulted, but we got no witnesses and no marks on him. And Mr. Budge here wants to file charges for trespassing. I say it's a wash and we wrap it up."

That's when I knew for sure that Officer Bill was on my side so I asked, "What about this guy using our address on his business cards?"

Flynn said, "I don't give a shit about none o' dat. It's a civil violation. Take it up in court."

"So what's it gonna be, gentlemen?" said Bill. "Both of you down to the station, or you both go home?"

I didn't have to think about it. "I'm happy to just go home and forget the whole thing." I already knew I would have hell to pay when I got home, and in the morning. "Just take this guy with you when you leave, all right? He's not welcome here."

Bill looked at Alejandro and said, "Well, what's it gonna be?"

"I have to show properties here. They can't deny me access."

Flynn got up in his face. "If I were you, laddie, I'd get my ass outta here now before we drag it out, get my drift?" Then he ripped up this Alejandro dude's business card and tossed it on the floor.

"Fine," he said. "I'm leaving." Then he looked over Flynn's shoulder at me and said, "But, we're not finished."

To which I replied, "Yeah, you're finished, bro."

"All right, let's go, Alejandro," said Bill. Then he turned to me and said, "Do you have a business card or something, for our records?"

"Sure," and I handed him one.

"Hey, Flynn, this guy actually lives here <u>and</u> works here. At least he's got the proper address on his card."

He then bent down and picked up the two halves of Alejandro's business card, handed it to me and winked. "For *your* records, eh? See ya 'round."

"Thanks office. Can I go home now?" I asked.

"Yeah, beat it."

The cops turned and headed for the entrance with Alejandro in tow. When his turn came to go through the revolver, Alejandro turned to look at me. I couldn't resist the temptation, so I gave him the finger. Too bad officer Bill was behind him. He never got a chance flip me back.

❧❧❧

"The guy was being a dick!"

"That doesn't give you the right to punch him out, Harry," Stan Lavine said.

As predicted, I was summoned to the management office by Alan at about 9:30 AM. Of course, after I got home the night before, I had to endure relentless ragging from Kathy about what a dumbass I am, how I needed anger management counseling, how I'd be lucky if I didn't lose my job, blah, blah, blah.

Word travels pretty fast around the building, thanks in large part to the doormen. So, when I got the call over the radio, I pretty much knew what to expect.

When I entered the office, Alan, Stan, and Jim McKenzie, the current board president (and incidentally, one of my biggest fans), were waiting. The seat of honor had been reserved for me, but it was getting hot.

"Look. The guy was photographing the lobby without permission.

When I asked him to either produce a consent form or leave, he started giving me lip. You want me to protect the property or what?"

"Yes we do," said Jim. "But we're not a housing project here. Sometimes, you have to use a little finesse."

"And you don't have the right to go smacking people around whenever you feel like it," Stan interjected.

"Yeah, yeah, I know. I heard you the first time." I was starting to get defensive.

"Take it easy, Harry. What are we going to do if this guy wants to sue the Association?" Jim asked.

"I seriously doubt that's going to happen," I grumbled.

"I wouldn't be so sure about that. We've been sued for a lot less," Alan interjected. He was referring to an incident that occurred when a piece of ice fell off the building and clobbered some woman. We beat that one -- "Act of God," and all that.

"Why don't you guys go to his web page," I said.

"What's that got to do with anything?" Stan snapped.

I threw Alejandro's torn business card, which I had taped back together, onto Alan's desk. "Check it out. I did."

Jim picked up the card and read it. "Why does he have our address on his card?"

"Go to his web page, like I said, and you tell me what's up," I replied.

Stan said to Alan, "Get online and go to the address on his card."

Alan fired up his computer and typed in the address from the business card. When the page came up, the wall paper was a picture of the Hancock. They all looked at each other; then they looked at me.

I said, "If you like that, then you'll love the rest. Go ahead, surf around and see what you think."

They all huddled over the computer and went from one photo of the property to another. Pics of the pool, the market, the fitness center, even the locker rooms. You would think the guy was the developer of the property. Conspicuously, however, there were no photos of an apartment interior. Not one. Then they got to his bio page.

"This guy makes himself sound like Mr. Hancock," said Jim, incredulously. "Alan, has this guy ever requested permission to take these photos, much less post them on the web?"

"Not to my knowledge, Jim. He certainly hasn't paid any fees. Anyway, all requests of that nature must go to the board directly for approval."

"How ya like me now?" I asked, smugly.

They all looked at me, but nobody said anything until Stan asked, "Alan, has this guy ever even listed anything in the building?"

"No way! I've never even heard of this guy before." It was Alan's job to review all sales documents, since the Association was entitled to first right of refusal as well as to collect a fee for processing. He knew all the agents who lived in the building, as well. Then he said, "Let me ask around and see if anybody knows this guy."

"I told you, this guy is a scam artist. I didn't intend for things to get out of hand; I was just trying to do my job," I offered apologetically.

Jim got up and closed the door. Since our meeting started, others had come into the main office. "Harry, I appreciate your dedication to the property, we all do. But you know there will be consequences. There are people here who will want to burn you at the stake."

"Yeah, I know," was all I could say.

"There's just one thing I'd like you to tell me before I decide what to do with you," he stated, and let it hang out there for a minute, with a solemn look on his face.

I figured the hammer was coming down. Instead, he cracked a smile and said, "Tell me the truth. How'd it feel to kick the little weasel's ass?"

⁂

As I left the office, Jim, Alan, and Stan assured me that they would all support me through whatever came of what we now referred to as "The Incident."

It wasn't long before the rumors began to fly. The anti-Harry faction, which I had long ago come to refer to as the "The Posse," started circulating the version that depicted me as a loose cannon that pummeled innocent real estate brokers for no good reason. Fortunately, that bunch was in the minority and was basically made up of misfits and malcontents whom nobody listened to anyway.

Another group consisting of more level headed residents, including several board members and real estate agents, came to my defense.

Apparently, this jackass, Alejandro, was well known and equally reviled in real estate circles as some kind of renegade. Turns out he had a reputation for sleazy dealing and undercutting other agents by shaving half the standard rate off his commission. He had never listed or sold a unit in the Hancock.

Soon, the "friendlies" would stop me and say things like, "We're all behind you, Harry."

One agent, Marge, took me aside and said, "That guy's a real jerk. I wish I were a man so I could splatter his face!" Coming from an older woman, it sounded comical. Evidently, there is honor among thieves (as well as real estate agents) and Alejandro had violated the code.

Some of the male residents would put up their dukes whenever they saw me and say, "How's it going, slugger?"

The crew, of course, showed a whole new level of respect for me. They were amazed that I had wiggled out of the whole mess without getting canned. So was I.

Alejandro, on the other hand, didn't fare so well. The Association filed a suit and forced him to shut down his web page. The only time we ever saw him again, he was apparently there to show a unit to a prospective buyer.

Fred, Sergei, and I were in an elevator going down when it stopped at a landing and in walked Alejandro with a multiple listing sheet in his hand.

"Hey, this is the guy, fellas," I said as I nodded at him. "How's it hangin'?" I said to him directly. "Guess that phone call didn't work out the way ya planned, huh?" He didn't say anything, but just turned and looked straight ahead as the doors closed.

"He don't look that tough to me," Fred said.

"Yeah, it is a good thing for him that he did not try to mess with Boomer," snickered Sergei with a slight Serbian accent. Sergei took English seriously and never used contractions, like Commander Data, the android, from *Star Trek-The Next Generation*. He talked the way he worked, with precision. Sometimes he got really anal with the minutiae though, which is why the crew dubbed him Sir Gay.

Old Alejandro just kept looking at the doors until they opened on 44 and everyone got out.

"Catch ya later, bro," I called after him, but he just kept walking toward the elevators that went to street level, and we never saw him again. Apparently, our property became a little too hot for him to handle.

Despite all attempts to quell the gossip, my legend continued to grow. The more I tried to downplay the incident, the bigger the story got. Eventually the commonly accepted story was that I had averted a major breach of security.

People refused to take my tamed down version of events as anything more than false modesty. Or in the case of "The Posse;" a lie designed to cover my own butt.

Finally, I resigned myself to just go with it. With regard to the majority of the residents, if they wished to think of me as their own personal super hero, I could live with that. In this business, when it comes to "atta-boys," you take what you can get. As far as "The Posse" was concerned, I figured it wouldn't hurt to let them believe I was a psychopath; maybe they'd stop screwing with me. What the heck, I thought. Sometimes, a bad reputation, to paraphrase Martha Stewart, can be a "very good thing."

The Great Newspaper Caper

"Mr. Budge, this is the fourth time in two weeks that you have reported not receiving your newspaper," said the woman on the phone. She seemed pleasant enough, but I didn't like the way the conversation was going. "Our records indicate that the paper was indeed delivered each time and that subsequent to your calls, a second delivery was also made."

"Yes, I did receive the later deliveries, but unfortunately, by the time I received the papers, it was too late to do me any good," I replied.

I had been receiving home delivery of the Chicago Tribune for years. Kathy had gotten me a subscription for my birthday one year and had kept it current. Like most high rise residences, home delivery meant that the paper was left on the floor outside your entry door early each morning.

The delivery personnel would sign in with the doorman at around 5:00 AM. So, by 8:00 AM., I could be having a cup of coffee and reading the front page at my desk. I would remove the crossword puzzle, fold it up and tuck it in my pocket for break time.

At first, I just though a mistake had been made. On the weekends when the papers weren't piled up outside my door on Sunday evening when I returned from Kathy's house, I assumed the janitors had picked them up. We didn't like to let them accumulate in the corridors, and had I told the weekend staff that they could have them rather than throw them away.

But recently, my paper was missing several days a week, and I was starting to get irritated. Even though the Tribune always sent a paper out when I complained, like I said to the lady at the delivery office, I didn't need the paper at 4:30 PM.

"I want my paper in the *morning,*" I restated.

"Yes, I understand, Mr. Budge. But as I've said, we have been delivering your paper every day, on time."

"So what are you saying, then?" I queried.

"Well, I obviously can't say with authority, since I don't have proof. But my guess is someone is stealing your paper."

"You're kidding, right? You mean to tell me that you think people who can afford to live in this building would resort to pilfering a fifty-cent newspaper on a routine basis?"

Even before I finished saying it, I knew she was right. It had to be the answer. What frosted me was that someone had the nerve to keep putting the snatch on *my* paper. I mean, I could see a one-time grab. But it took balls to continue hitting the same apartment repeatedly, with no apparent fear of being caught.

"Mr. Budge, trust me when I tell you, this is not at all uncommon. We receive hundreds of calls a day concerning theft of newspapers. And I mean from luxury high rises to houses all over the city. It is such a problem that we have a special office dedicated to dealing with it."

"Well, what can you do about it?" I asked.

"Not much," She said, "unless the thief is actually caught in the act. If that happens, then the Tribune will aggressively pursue prosecution. Keep in mind we take newspaper theft seriously, since home delivery accounts for a substantial amount of sales. People will not subscribe if we can't reasonably guarantee delivery."

"So, if I catch him, then…"

"You can call either us or the police or both. Then the person will be prosecuted," she finished for me.

"Well, thank you, Marie. You've been very helpful, given the circumstances. I appreciate your advice."

"My pleasure, Mr. Budge. I am sorry that you have to deal with this," she offered.

"Don't you worry 'bout a thing, Marie. I'm gonna catch this guy, and when I do, I'm calling back and asking for you, okay?"

"I'll be happy to help in any way I can. Goodbye."

"Can you believe it?" I was talking to Alan about the purloining of my paper. "The audacity! I mean, it takes balls to keep ripping off the same guy, you know?"

"Yeah, no kidding. So what do you think you're going to do about it?" he wanted to know.

"Well, somehow I've got to catch this guy. I just don't think I've got the patience to sit like a deer hunter, waiting for prey. I'd have to get up at five and sit with my ear to the door for God knows how long. And whoever it is; he isn't taking it every morning. So, who knows how many days I'd have to wait to catch him?"

"Well, whatever you do, if you nab the guy, don't hit him, okay?" Alan said, half joking/half seriously. "You got lucky last time." Of course he was referring to the Alejandro deal.

"Yeah, yeah, I hear you loud and clear. If and when I catch the little snake, I'll come to you first."

"That's good," he said. "Hey, I have an idea. Can you use that covert camera gear we have?"

I thought about it for second and said, "I can't believe I didn't think of that before. I could set it up with the recorder in my kitchen.

The camera is wireless and can be run on batteries, so there won't be any wiring exposed to give it away. I like it. That's awesome!"

"Well, go get it from the closet, then," he prodded.

Alan and I had a standing agreement. The equipment was stored in his closet in a locked suitcase, but the key was kept in my office key safe. We both had been around in the business long enough to understand the value of protecting ourselves. There had been incidents reported around the city in the past of unscrupulous building managers and/or engineers being accused of covert voyeurism in other properties. Therefore, we both thought it prudent to provide ourselves with, for lack of a better term, "Plausible Deniability." I'd snagged that phrase from some news byte concerning Oliver North in the eighties or something.

"Okay. So you're writing down the reason I'm using the equipment, right?" I asked.

"Yeah, I gotcha covered. It's legit. We would do it for anybody else. Just keep a record for yourself as well. Just the details like when you checked it out, where the camera and recorder are going to be located, what you're expecting to record, etc. That should do it."

"Alrighty, then," I said as I started to leave. "In the immortal words of Sherlock Holmes, 'the game is afoot!'"

I was all wired up when I left Alan's office (no pun intended). I couldn't wait to get the gear set up and catch the little creep who was ripping me off. Of course, as with most men over forty, video equipment was not my strongest forte. I could troubleshoot and repair almost any kind of machinery, perform carpentry and masonry with reasonable proficiency, or calculate and set the optimum water pressure for any size facility. But sadly, programming a VCR was a challenge. Not a shortcoming I was likely to acknowledge either.

With this in mind, I went to my place and set about mounting the camera in an inconspicuous location first. I would deal with the actual recording device later. The camera itself was a very small digital component which was black in color (the color of the door and frame). The fact that my entry door was located at the end of the corridor, sort of in the shadows, was quite beneficial. I installed two new AAA batteries in the case that supplied power to the camera via a tiny lead, and mounted the unit to the door closer. It was hard to see, even if I pointed it out. Perfect!

Now; on to step two.

I set up the receiver and monitor in my kitchen, which was only steps from the entry door. After acquiring the camera signal, I had to set the unit for the best angle and picture quality. That part wasn't that hard, just time consuming. I didn't want any assistance, in order to reduce the chance of a leak which would scare off my quarry. I had learned from experience that when it came to trying to catch somebody doing something wrong, the fewer people who knew about it, the better.

I laid an old newspaper on the floor outside the door, in the approximate target zone the paper boy had arbitrarily chosen for my daily delivery; a spot in the middle of the corridor about eight feet short of my door. He never failed. Always hit the same place. I locked myself out once, trying to run, grab the paper, and get back to the door before it slammed shut. Trust me when I say, it's no fun being locked out of your apartment, when all you have on is your pajama bottoms, even if you are a stud-muffin like me.

Anyway, since the camera was mounted to the door closer, which was in turn mounted to the door, I would have to make an adjustment and then wait for the door to completely close before I could critique the subsequent view. So it took some time. But finally, I was zeroed in. I had a perfectly clear view of about sixty square feet outside my door, including my neighbor, Alice's, entry door.

Next step; connecting the recorder.

The thing was totally digital. No tapes, therefore, no rewinding. No running out of recording media. It was designed to record continuously for seven days, and then rerecord over the oldest time frames. FIFO was what the nerds called it. First in, first out.

The wiring was simple. After verifying that all the cables from the power source to the recorder, from the recorder to the monitor, and from the receiver to both the monitor and the recorder were properly connected, I was ready for the final and most difficult step: programming.

Now, I've always liked puzzles. I even like video games -- mostly, the kind where you're shooting aliens all over the place and searching for treasure. But this kind of programming thing was more like torture. The book never makes sense until after you screw up about a half dozen times on every step! It took about two hours of trial and error, but after repeated tests, I was pretty sure I had it.

I recorded myself in the corridor several times and played it back on the small portable monitor.

Just when I was ready to claim victory and let her rip, I noticed that the date stamp was off by about a year and two months. Damn! I would have to go through all that crap again to set the time and date. Without that information, anything I recorded would be useless when the culprit was finally caught. I intended to go for the maximum when I nailed the scoundrel, so I wanted the evidence to be indisputable.

I suffered through another half hour of button pushing and verifying, undoing and redoing, when finally, I really was ready. I set the equipment to standby, since it was still the middle of the day, and went to work. With high hopes, I started the recorder that night before I went to bed.

THE GREAT NEWSPAPER CAPER

I awoke on Friday morning at around 6:30 AM. I must have been a bit keyed up, since I didn't usually get up until around seven-thirty, unless I planned to work out at the fitness center. I headed toward the kitchen to make some coffee before getting ready for work. Before I got there, I stopped in the entry foyer and opened the door to see if the paper was there. It was there all right, not in its usual spot, halfway down the hall, but right in front of the door. Too bad, I thought. Not this time. No matter. Based on the established pattern, the thief would strike again, sooner or later. I and my camera would be ready and waiting.

I left the paper where it was (I usually just picked it up on the way to the office) and went to make my coffee. While it was brewing, I rewound the recorder to view the previous night's activity. I cued the recording to around 5:00 AM. No paper at 5:13 AM.

At about 5:18 AM, my newspaper landed in its usual spot. I couldn't see the paper boy which told me he was tossing it from somewhere down the hall. So that's why it never makes it to my door, I thought. Interesting. I fast forwarded to 6:14 AM. That's when I saw Alice leave her place dressed for a workout. She stopped as she was passing my paper and looked down for a second. Then she kicked it two or three times until it settled where I found it, in front of my door.

Well, that explains that. I'd have to thank Alice when I saw her.

I got up and went to the battery box for the camera which hung inside the door. I flipped the switch to off, in the interest of conserving power. I had discovered that the batteries ran down quickly on those digital cameras if you left them on continuously.

I sat down to watch the news and some of the Today show while I drank my coffee. At about 7:30 AM, I showered, shaved and got dressed.

Imagine my disbelief when I left the apartment at eight, and discovered that my newspaper had once again evaporated. Likewise, to my chagrin, I realized I had turned off the power to the camera less than an hour previously! Man, was I pissed.

Well, after moping around all day long over missing the "catch of the day," I went home and reworked the video equipment. After fiddling around most of the evening, I had finally connected an AC/DC converter to the camera so that I could run the system 24/7. Taking the batteries out of the equation meant there was no reason to turn the system off until the trap was sprung, so to speak.

I checked and rechecked the operation until I was satisfied that everything worked perfectly. Now it was all about being patient. Turned out, I didn't have long to wait.

The next morning, I decided to start my day with a workout. When the alarm went off at 6:00 AM, I got up, got dressed, and headed down to the fitness center. My paper was again close to the door (I assumed Alice had done me another favor) so I decided to let it ride until I returned, just to see if the thief would go for it.

I grabbed some coffee at the office on the way down. The midnight shift probably made it around 12:00 AM, so it was a little muddy, but drinkable. When I walked in I saw Alice and walked on over to thank her for kicking my paper over to my door.

"Hi Alice," I said as I approached. She didn't hear me, since she was listening to her Ipod while she worked the weights.

She must have seen my lips moving so she stopped what she was doing, removed her ear buds and said, "Oh, hi Harry. I'm sorry. I didn't hear you."

"I was just saying hello. But I also wanted to thank you for kicking my paper back in front of my door the last couple of days. I appreciate it"

"You're welcome. I know it's yours since we're the only ones down at the end of the hall. But how did you know it was me?"

Dummy. I hadn't anticipated that question. I mulled it over in my head briefly and realized that if she had been the guilty party, she would have taken my paper rather than moving it closer to my door. So I opted to tell her what I was up to.

"Well, to tell you the truth, I've got some surveillance equipment set up to watch my entrance."

"Why?" she asked, with raised eyebrows. "What's going on?"

I proceeded to tell her about my being victimized and how it was becoming an almost daily occurrence.

"Really, I had no idea. I've never seen anyone in our hallway that didn't live here. My Wall Street Journal has never been stolen."

I opted not to mention that I could see why (yawn) no one would steal *her* paper.

Anyway, I finished my story, excused myself and proceeded with my work out. I finished up with a couple miles on the treadmill, and headed back up to my apartment at about 7:00 AM.

As I rounded the corner from the elevator lobby to my corridor I could see all the way down to my door. That's when I knew I hit the jackpot. My newspaper was missing once again! I literally dashed to my door and went straight to the recorder.

I cued the recording first to about 6:15 AM, since I knew the paper was still there when I left. There I was, walking out the door, paper on the floor. I then fast forwarded until I saw a flash of color, and then the paper was gone. The time stamp said 6:47 AM. I then rewound back to 6:45 AM and played it at normal speed. After about a minute, here he came.

First, I saw an unrecognizable head stick out from the doorway to the service corridor which ran behind the apartment. This is where the laundry rooms, freight elevators, and trash chutes are located on every floor. The service corridors run perpendicular to the two residential corridors, which run parallel to each other from east to west. I lived on the north corridor, west end. Picture a ladder with the two residential corridors representing the rails of the ladder with the two service corridors and the elevator lobby as the three rungs.

I watched the head look first right then left (toward my door), and then the perp walked right over to my paper, bent down and picked it up. And without knowing it, looked directly into the camera.

I was floored. I had to replay the sequence half a dozen times to be sure. There was no doubt. The thief was not a he, but rather a she -- none other than my neighbor from the south corridor, Lucy Gable. She was hard to mistake. Five feet tall, huge bubble butt, bottle blonde hair, wearing the red Japanese designer bathrobe that she always wore around when she was dumping garbage or doing laundry, and of course, those hideous Harry Carey glasses with the saucer-sized lenses.

There she was, prancing right up to my door like she owned the place and walking away with my paper.

I couldn't believe it. This was a woman who had been living there as long as I had, and whom I conversed with regularly in the laundry room or in the elevators. I had even done some side work for her in the past and only charged her half of what I would have charged anyone else, trying to be neighborly. This was how she repaid my kindness?

I began thinking of other unexplained incidents involving missing property. Kathy and I once had several brand-new beach towels stolen right out of the dryer. I'd forgotten about it until that moment.

Whoever did the stealing actually rifled through our laundry and took only the new towels and left the rest. I was sure now that Miss Lucy was the felon.

With effort, I forced myself to resist the urge to stomp over to her door and confront her. I decided I needed to consult with Alan before I proceeded further. Besides, I wanted him to confirm her identification. I might have been wrong, but I sure didn't think so. No way, no how! It was her all right. I had proof. The only question was what to do with it. It didn't take me long to decide.

⁓⁓⁓

"That's her, Harry," Alan said after ten seconds of viewing the video.

Prior to bringing Alan up to my place, I had connected the recorder to my big screen TV, so it would be easier to view. The little 5 inch monitor, I thought, might make the details harder to discern.

"Damn right that's her," said Fred. I wanted a third opinion so I invited Fred to watch the show as well. "I'd recognize that booty anywhere!"

"You guys have no doubt, right?"

"I sure don't," chimed Fred.

"No. It's definitely her," averred Alan with a laugh. "I never told you this one, but they caught her stealing meat in the market on 44."

"You're full of it!" I exclaimed. I was sure he was just yankin' my chain.

"No, I'm not," Alan protested. "The store operators caught her red handed about three months ago. And I also have it on authority that she was caught shop lifting at Lord and Taylor."

"What? Is this chick a klepto or something?"

"Evidently. She certainly doesn't need to be stealing. She got her condo free and clear in a divorce and she has a good job. She must be sick."

"Well personally, I don't care what her problems are. She's been ripping me off for months now and I want restitution."

"Well, how do you want to handle it then?" Alan asked.

I thought it over for a minute. I was really pissed off. Particularly so since the notion had entered my mind that she thought she could screw me over with impunity because I was an employee. I guess that's when I decided it was time little Miss Lucy learned a thing or two about messing with me.

"Are you willing to handle it, Alan?"

"Sure -- what do you want me to do?"

"Tell her she can either pay me back for a full quarter of home delivery or I'm contacting the police and the Tribune and let them deal with her the way they do all thieves." A part of me really wanted her to turn down the offer.

───

"She claims that today was the only time she has ever taken your newspaper," Alan said as I entered his office. "I told her I'd talk to you."

"Yeah, right. And my ass turns green on St. Patrick's Day! Look, there's no room for compromise, Alan. I'm not kidding. Either I get $45.00 cash or I call the cops. Nothing in between. She's got until tomorrow, at four.

"All right, I'll let her know. You want me to call her now? You can stay here if you want."

"Yeah, sure," I said. I really wanted to listen to this.

Alan dialed Lucy's work number and asked for her when the operator answered. When she came on the line, Alan said, "Hello Ms. Gable. This is Alan Kane at 175 E. Delaware Place." Of course

I couldn't hear what she said back so I just sat there and listened to Alan's side of the conversation.

"I've spoken to Harry and he is adamant that you pay him for a full quarter of home delivery service or he is going forward with the police report."

Silence.

Then, "That doesn't matter to him. And I suspect it won't matter to the police. One time is as bad as a hundred, and you're the one he has on tape. Furthermore, Harry is a resident and as such is entitled to the same respect and protections as all other residents."

Presumably she was protesting, expecting Alan to forbid me to have a resident prosecuted. After all, I was merely a servant.

"Well, I've told you what he wants. Now it's up to you. If he doesn't have $45.00 by 4:00 PM tomorrow, he says he's calling the police. It's out of my hands. I'm sorry."

Pause.

"Thank you. Goodbye. Oh, and have a nice day." Alan hung up the phone with a devious smile on his face.

"She keeps claiming she only took your paper this one time, and that this whole incident is being blown way, way out of proportion. I know she's lying. The first time I spoke to her she told me she only took it one other time when you were on vacation. I asked her how she knew if you were on vacation. Then she tried to backtrack, and changed the story again. You heard me tell her you don't care what her story is and the cops won't care how many times she took it. Guilty is as guilty does!"

"I guess we'll wait and see," I said. "I'll let you know what happens." Then I got up and left the management office. I intended to get satisfaction, one way or another.

I finished up the work day at 4:30 PM as usual. I was just settling in to watch a rerun of "The X-Files" when the phone rang. Looking at the caller ID screen I saw the number appear after the name L. Gable. I had no desire to speak to Lucy; I just wanted my money. I was also irritated that she had the nerve to call me at home. She would have had to get my number from information since, for obvious reasons, I didn't throw my home number around casually in the building. Anyway, I let it go into voice mail.

After watching TV for around half an hour, curiosity got the best of me and I called my voice mail. After entering my security code and going into new messages, I began listening to what would turn out to be a twenty minute proclamation of innocence intertwined with a lame attempt at an apology from Lucy. She droned on and on about how she had never taken my paper before, how she was having a really bad morning and needed the paper to line her bird's cage and that she intended to replace my paper, blah, blah, blah. As if reading today's paper tomorrow or the next day would have certainly made up for everything.

Needless to say, I wasn't buying any of it. The more she blabbed, the more I knew she was lying. You can just tell, you know? Nothing she said was ever going to change my mind. I finally had enough and deleted the message then hung up the phone. I resumed watching the tube and ate a TV dinner. Kathy called around 9:00 PM.

"So how was your day?" she asked when I answered the phone.

"Verrry interrresting and quite frrruitful. Mmmwahahahaha!" I was doing my best dastardly evil guy impression as I proceeded to relate the results of my sting operation.

"You're kidding. I can't believe it was her all this time." Kathy was privy to the entire saga since I was bitching about it all the time.

It had been going on for months and frankly, she was getting tired of hearing me rag about it every other morning. I told her of the ultimatum I had Alan present to Lucy, and I think she was relieved that I might soon be out of her misery.

"So now we'll see if she pays up or I turn her in," I said in closing.

"Well, good luck with that." Kathy was always skeptical of my schemes. "Don't be surprised if she blows you off."

"If she does, she'll regret it," I stated firmly.

"Whatever."

I almost wished Lucy would refuse to pay. It was now more a matter of pride than an issue of the money. I never let anybody screw me over and get away with it. Kathy and I chatted a little while longer; then we said good night.

The next day I awoke at the usual time and set about my morning routine. Before jumping in the shower, I walked over to the entrance foyer and opened the door to get my newspaper.

Although the paper was in its usual spot, down the hall, there at my threshold was a plain white envelope. After, ensuring my latch was in the unlocked position, I reached down for the envelope, retrieved my paper and re-entered the apartment.

I sat down at the dining room table and picked up the envelope. It was sealed but had no writing whatsoever on the outside. I ripped it open and out fell two twenty dollar bills and a five. That was it. No note. No indication of where it came from or who had left it.

Of course, it was obvious that Lucy was my mysterious benefactor. But even in this act of atonement, she had found a way to show her contempt. By not addressing the envelope or inserting an apology letter, she was not accepting responsibility for what she had done. She was merely avoiding the consequences for her actions.

I considered keeping the money and turning her in anyway, but that would amount to sacrificing my honor. A deal is a deal, I figured, and I never stated that a written apology was required. Too late, I realized that if you barter with the devil, it is the letter of the bargain, not the spirit, which ultimately prevails.

✦✦✦

I left the surveillance equipment in place for several weeks after nailing Lucy, on the off chance that she was telling the truth and that there really was a second paper-taker. Not! My newspaper was never stolen again.

I eventually tired of tripping over the power cord for the camera and of the electronics all over the kitchen counter, so I dismantled the spy station and returned the equipment to the management office.

Lucy and I rarely met after that. I actually took the stairs to work for a while to avoid being alone in an elevator with her. You'd think that I was the guilty party! I just did not want to open the door to any more of her phoney-baloney apologies or lame explanations.

Well, I needn't have worried. On the occasions when we did meet, the tension was so thick you could cut it with a knife. She never attempted to start a conversation of any kind and neither did I.

Lucy eventually sold her place, and moving day arrived. I remember hearing her arguing with her movers in the service corridor. She was complaining about how long they were taking. They were protesting that the freight elevator was holding them up. Actually, I had taken one of the two freight cars out of service for maintenance, which meant that we could not allow her exclusive service for her move since everyone else would have to share the remaining elevator.

Of course, movers charge by the hour so her bill was getting higher and higher every minute they were standing around waiting. What a drag. If only I'd realized that taking an elevator out of service would have caused her such an expensive hardship; I might have scheduled the maintenance for another day, but I don't think so. Mmmwwahahahaha!

Water, Weenies and Wackos

I know, the expression, "it's not rocket science," is getting really tired from overuse but, plumbing ain't rocket science! However, I can assure you that it is quite possible to turn a rocket scientist, or any other egg-head for that matter, into a blithering idiot by simply adding water.

)))(

I like to compare systems in residential buildings to systems in the human body. Like a body, buildings require circulatory systems (domestic water distribution), waste systems (sewage and trash removal), respiratory systems (ventilation), etc.

As in the human body, the circulatory system is complicated. Just as a blood clot may cause circulation problems in arteries or a drop in blood flow to extremities, a similar blockage in a re-circulating line will cause a lack of hot water, a lack of pressure, or both. A blockage in a waste line is like, well, an unpleasant situation under any circumstance.

Actually, plumbing issues require the lion's share of attention in any residential high-rise building. And as irritating as it may be, every high-rise dweller soon learns that temporary suspension of water service, for a variety of reasons, is a common occurrence.

A shutdown in the Hancock typically affected twelve apartments in the same vertical tier. Sometimes two tiers (twenty-four apartments) would be affected if, say, the kitchens were back-to-back. Twelve floors are about the maximum you can have in one plumbing zone due the pressure differential between the top floor and the bottom floor. The pressure increases about 4.3 psi per floor as you head down the tier. Therefore, if the minimum pressure is 40 psi at the top floor, then the pressure at the bottom would be at least 90 psi. Any pressure higher than that would be considered unsuitable for a variety of reasons. Okay, that's it for today's plumbing lesson.

Well, one Tuesday, the guys were preparing to shut down the domestic water for the 05 tier of apartments in the middle -high zone (62nd floor thru 71st floor) so that a remodeling contractor could change valves in 6405. This was a simple matter for the crew since they performed shutdowns regularly, due to the frequency of remodeling and/or repairs which were constantly underway.

Whenever we scheduled a shutdown, we sent memos out to alert the residents of the affected apartments. There are few things worse than being halfway through a morning shower and having the water pressure suddenly diminish to a trickle. And there's nothing worse than being me when a resident wants to slap the crap out of me following such an occurrence.

Nevertheless, there were always residents who failed to read the memos slipped under their doors, so I was used to hearing complaints, regardless of how much advance notice we provided. Just to be safe, we always waited until after 9:00 AM before securing the water service.

"Call me when you're done, guys. I want to get busy with the air handlers," I told Donny and Sergei.

"No problem, chief," said Sergei. "We will call you when we are done so we can help you fill the coils."

It was late April and I had planned to put the cooling coils in

WATER, WEENIES AND WACKOS

the big air handlers back in service that day. We always drained the coils in the fall to prevent freezing and subsequent ruptures during the winter. The forecast was calling for high temperatures by the end of the week, and I wanted to be prepared.

"All right," I said. "I'll catch ya later," and they were on their way.

Before long, I heard the guys on the radio going through their routine as usual. One of them would shut down the hot and cold supply valves at the top of the tier, and the other would shut down the hot water return valve at the bottom. Then one guy would enter the apartment at the bottom of of the affected tier, to drain the risers (in this case, 6205). The other guy would vent the air from the risers by opening the taps in the apartment at the top of the tier. Venting allows the water to drain freely and quickly.

Usually it took a couple of hours from start to finish. After shutting down the water and verifying the flow had in fact stopped, the crew would notify the contractors that it was safe to proceed, or in some cases, perform the work themselves. When the work was complete they would notify the service desk and proceed to reverse the process to restore water pressure, inspect for leaks, and that would be that. No big deal… most of the time.

⁂

"Harry, this chick is really starting to be a pain," Fred was saying as he walked into my office. He was holding a work order in his hand. "We've been up to her place about a half dozen times to clear the toilet, but she keeps clogging it up again."

"Who is she?" I asked as I took the work order from his hand.

"She's the daughter of the owners, Mr. and Mrs. Carlyle, and she's been using the place for a couple of weeks while she's home from college. She's basically a pretty nice girl, cute too. But she's starting to complain about all the service calls."

The work order was for apartment 8103, which, I recalled from memory, was an in-town get away for a middle-aged married couple from Indiana.

There had been a new trend in vacation properties sweeping through the market for a while. Rather than the traditional scenario where a family lived and worked in the city and bought a summer cottage on a lake somewhere in Michigan or Wisconsin, it was kind of reversed. Increasingly, many baby-boomers opted to live in the suburbs and purchase second homes in downtown high-rises.

Many times, these absentee owners would allow friends or family members to use the apartment for a weekend or longer. Of course, these guests would somehow think they were staying in a hotel and mistakenly believe that we provided hotel services. The guests didn't understand that everything we did inside a unit resulted in a service charge. Once people knew they had to pay, they generally called us as a last resort.

"What seems to be the problem?" I asked.

"We don't know. Every time one of the guys goes up, they use a plunger or an auger to clear the toilet. It flushes fine and they leave. The next time she uses it, it clogs up again."

"Sounds to me like something's stuck in the trap," I offered. Dropping foreign objects into the toilet is as old, as...well, as old as toilets! I've seen all kinds of things removed from toilet traps. Pens, eyeglasses, toys, you name it. Even a wallet once, complete with credit cards and driver's license. The problem is that in the case of something like a comb or a pen, the toilet won't clog unless there is a lot of paper or solid waste introduced. Eeeew!

What usually happens then is that the auger or plunger will clear the bowl, but the object will stay lodged crosswise in the throat of the trap. This allows water to pass, and the toilet flushes fine until the next time someone actually uses it, at which time, it clogs up

WATER, WEENIES AND WACKOS

again. In the end, the only way to resolve the issue is to lift the toilet, turn it over and manually remove the obstruction. This is why plumbers make a hundo and a half an hour!

Invariably, the resident disputes the charge for pulling the toilet to remove the offending object. So as disgusting as it may sound, I've instructed the crew to preserve the culprit as evidence to counter the owner's claim that they would "never allow anything to fall into the toilet." Of course the guy with the wallet didn't protest *his* bill.

"Well, you know what to do," I said to Fred as I handed the work order back to him. "Donny and Sir Gay can pull it after they're done with the shutdown for 6405."

"Yeah, they should be about done restoring pressure. I'll send them there next."

"Hey," I called after Fred as he was leaving. "Make sure they save whatever it is they pull out. She's probably already whining to Mommy and Daddy, and you know she's going to argue about what caused the problem."

"10-4," he said as he left.

About a half hour later, I was at my desk when the house phone rang. The screen showed the call was from 8103. "Engineering," I said as I put the phone to my ear.

"Harry, can you come up here for a minute? You gotta see this to believe it." It was Fred.

"Did they get the toilet up?"

"Yeah, they got it up all right. Like I said, you really gotta see this."

"All right, I'm on my way."

When I got to 8103 I called out, "Hello," as I entered.

"Back here, chief," came the reply from Donny. He, Fred and Sergei were in the guest bathroom, which was across the hall from the second bedroom.

"So, what's the story?" I asked as I walked up to the bathroom door. They had the toilet sitting in the hallway on a tarp and they were in the bathroom standing by the sink.

"What was stuck in the trap, a roll of twenties?" I figured it had to be good for them to insist I needed to see it.

"Not exactly -- check this out," said Donny, as he held up a huge carrot.

I didn't reach for it, for obvious reasons, but I said, "Very impressive. So what?" We had encountered instances of people trying to use their toilets as garbage disposals before. No big deal.

"No, man. Look closer!" blurted Fred.

Donny extended his latex gloved hand so that I could get a better look. Upon closer inspection, I could plainly see that the smaller end of the carrot had been carved into the shape of a circumcised penis. The craftsman spared no detail. The thing even appeared to have veins. The guys couldn't hold it back anymore and they started cracking up.

"I heard she was studying to be a chef," chuckled Fred.

"Must be a whole new way to get your veggies," quipped Donny.

"Maybe someone should have told her to have a V-8," interjected Sergei.

"Shut up, you guys! Is she around?" I didn't want the girl to overhear us.

"Nah. She said she was going down to the fitness center because she didn't want to be grossed out," said Donny.

"I'd love to see her face when she sees this," Fred chuckled.

It appeared he would get his wish, because just then, we heard the entry door squeak open. I told the guys to leave the carrot and follow me to the living room.

"Hello," I said as we all walked into the room. "You must be Miss Carlyle."

"Call me Carrie. Did you guys finally fix the toilet?"

She was twenty-something, blond of course, slim and fit looking in her designer gym outfit, and she seemed to have a nice disposition, which was unusual, based on our experience. We tended to encounter a lot of attitude with many of the residents' kids.

I casually glanced at the guys with my "keep your mouth shut and let me handle this" look. "Uh, yeah. As a matter of fact the guys removed a foreign object from the trap. Unfortunately, there will be a charge for the service today".

"Why? I don't understand why I should be charged for a problem with the plumbing," she protested.

"I'm sorry, miss, but the object they extracted was dropped in, accidentally, we presume, but not a building responsibility, regardless. Therefore, we'll have to charge you."

"What was it that was stuck down in there, then? I want to see it."

All right, you asked for it, I thought. "It's in the bathroom, on the sink."

As she headed off to the bathroom I looked over at the guys. Donny was grinning, with his arms folded, rocking back and forth on the balls of his feet. Sergei and Fred were just standing still, looking around the apartment. None of them said anything.

Suddenly, we heard a gasp and then all was quiet. After a minute or so, she came out and said, "Um, so what's the charge?" Her face had lost some of its color. In fact I would later refer to her hue as a "whiter shade of pale."

"Well," I said as I started computing, "by the time they reinstall the toilet, counting the new wax ring and two man hours of labor, it'll come to about one hundred and twenty-five dollars. We can just add it to the monthly assessment." That's when she started to squirm.

"Uh, no, I think I'll just pay for it now, if that's okay." She was practically pleading.

I had no desire to embarrass her further; I'm really not that mean. So I said, "You can take the yellow copy of the work order down to the bookkeeper, Dana, and she'll tell you what to do. But you must understand that the service charges will be submitted in a couple of days, so you need to take care of it soon or it will be assessed."

"No problem. I'll go down right now."

I completed filling in the work order which Fred had given me while she was in the bathroom (leaving out the specifics) and extended her the yellow copy. She took it from my hand and headed toward the entrance. Just before she went through the door she turned to me with a relieved look on her face, and mouthed "thank you."

After she left, I instructed the guys to bag the carrot and replace the toilet.

"If she comes back with a receipt, leave the carrot and the rest of the copies of the work order and get lost." She seemed like a nice girl, so I figured if we got the money, we wouldn't need the paper trail. I could make the original copy go away. No harm, no foul. "If not, take it with you. We might need the evidence later. She may be little hottie, but nobody gets a free ride."

I said to Fred as we left 8103, "You want to get something to eat? I'm starving." It was about 11:30 AM, and I was getting hungry, since

I never ate breakfast.

"Sounds good," said Fred.

So we headed down to the market on 44 for a sandwich. After we checked out I said, "Let's go to my place. I've got pop and chips. After lunch we can get started with the cooling coils, all right?"

"Cool. Maybe we can eat lunch in peace for a change," he replied.

If we ate in the office we would no doubt be answering our phones every five minutes. If we ate in the locker room/lunch room with the guys, then we'd have to listen to them argue about their card game. They played cards together at lunch every day and they were all shameless cheaters.

We had just sat down at my dining room table when Mandy called Fred on the radio. "Delaware Two, come in please."

"Come back," he replied as he started taking his food out of the bag.

"We have a report of a leak coming through the ceiling in apartment 6705," Mandy relayed.

"10-4," answered Fred

"What did Ennis and Penis screw up now," I said to Fred with an accusatory tone. Of course, I was referring to Donny and Sergei. The reported leak was in the same tier where they had performed the water shutdown earlier.

"Nothing, Harry. I swear. I checked the work myself before they restored pressure," he protested.

"It wouldn't be the first time they forgot to close the taps in an apartment they were draining or venting from," I declared. "You better get your ass up there and check it out right now, dude."

"Fine, I'm going already," he said as he left the table.

"Get the twins busy up there as soon as they're done with 8103. Call me when you track it down. I'll put your food in the fridge."

"Thanks a lot," he said with a hint of disgust as he walked out the door.

I had no intention of skipping my lunch to chase down a leak which I was convinced would turn out to be our fault. It was bad enough I would have to deal with the fallout, and Fred understood that. I took the heat, he did the leg work.

Whenever we received a report of a leak, the guys would split up and check the floors in ascending order in the tier where the leak was reported. We'd always start at the apartment immediately above and work our way up until we discovered the source.

I heard Fred calling the other guys, all of them, on the radio a few minutes later.

"Delaware Two to all Delawares, report to apartment 6905 right away, and bring the wet vacs." Then, "Delaware One, come in."

"Come back, Fred," I replied.

"We found the source of the leak. Can you come to 6905?"

"10-4. I'll be right there." I didn't like to discuss details over the radio, since our radios were always on an open channel. You just never knew who might be listening. If you were me, would you want to broadcast all your screw-ups? Anyway, I left the apartment with what was left of my sandwich and headed for the high-rise.

When I got to the door of 6905, water had already found its way to the corridor. I finished the last bite of my ham and cheese as I walked into the apartment.

I was presented with what looked like a receding tsunami. There had to be at least two inches of water pooled up in the low spots. Someone had already constructed a makeshift dam of rags near the foyer, in order to contain the majority of the water within the apartment. The floor of the entire place was marble, so it resembled a draining swimming pool.

Wait a minute, I thought as I glanced around. I knew the guy that lived there. He was a CPA with Price-Waterhouse. "All right, what happened?" I asked Donny, who was the first one there.

"The taps in the bathroom were both wide open and the plug was in the drain," he replied.

"Show me."

I sloshed my way behind him into the only bathroom as he recounted what he had found. Meanwhile Fred kept busy directing the rest of the staff in the clean-up project.

The sink taps were the kind that protrude directly from the wall. The plug was indeed in the drain and the sink was full. The overflow ports on sinks and tubs are not intended to drain the full flow if the taps are left on when the plug is in, contrary to what most people believe. The intent is, for example, to drain away the excess in a tub that is filled too high when a person gets in.

The guys had already lifted the toilet, thereby creating a floor drain. This was a trick I had learned from the fire fighters and had subsequently taught to the crew.

"Did you guys send notices out to everybody in the tier?" I asked.

"Sure did," replied Fred. "In fact the one for this apartment is floating on the floor near the door."

I walked out of the bathroom and wove my way between the hoses, wet vacs and bodies toward the entrance. Sure enough, there was a sheet of paper on the floor. I picked it up and read it. It was the shutdown notice which had been slid under the door two days previously. Unfortunately, as is the case with much of the communication that is sent to the residents, it was left on the floor and disregarded.

By that time, it was obvious to me what had happened. We had encountered this sort of calamity far too many times in the past. Evidently the resident, who had never bothered to read the shutdown notice, tried to fill the sink after the risers had been drained.

Predictably, after finding neither hot nor cold water available, the guy walked away without closing the taps. So when the water pressure was restored the taps were in the fully open position and allowed to run, with the drain closed, overflowing and filling the apartment until such time as it leaked through the floor. In this case, it wasn't noticed until it had leaked down through two lower apartments.

It was not our policy to check every apartment in the tier after a shutdown. It was difficult enough gaining permission to enter the apartments required for draining and venting.

"What about 6805?" I asked.

Fred said. "Sir Gay says there's a lot of damage. The owners are pretty pissed."

"I'm sure they are. Well, get the water up as fast you can, then split the guys up between 6705 and 6805," I directed Fred. "And contact the resident of this place and tell him what happened."

"Aw, c'mon! Why do I have to do it? You know he's gonna be all pissed off and try to find a way to blame it on us."

"Tough. Stop being such a pussy." I loved to hear Fred snivel. I did feel his pain, but I figured it was time he learned what it was like to sit in the big chair.

"And document every man hour it takes to clean this mess up. I want it all charged back to the genius who lives here, including the clean-up of the other two apartments." I was turning to leave when I remembered 8103. "Hey, how'd things work out at 8103?"

"It's cool," said Donny. "She came back with a receipt so we left the work orders and the carrot, just like you said."

"Good." At least I have one good deed under my belt today, I thought. I felt better about having to add insult to injury by sending a bill to the bean counter. "I have other stuff to do now. I still want to work on the cooling coils if we get time, so call me when you're done." So far, I hadn't completed even one thing on my to-do list.

"Hey, what about lunch?" asked Tim.

"Lunch is canceled for you and anyone else who asks." I was just screwing with them. It would probably take them at least a couple of hours to clean up all three apartments.

"Get lunch when you're done, okay?" I said to them all. "I promise I won't dock any of you. Call when you're finished. Maybe we can get some real work done!"

It was about 1:30 PM and I was just finishing checking my voice mail when the radio squawked again.

"Delaware Two come in please." It was Mandy.

"Come back," came Fred's reply.

"We have a report of another leak in 5708."

Before Fred could respond, I called Mandy. "Service desk, come in."

"Come back."

"Mandy, this is Harry. I'll check this one out. The rest of the guys are tied up with the leak in the high-rise."

"10-4," she replied.

So far, the whole day was sucking. This was just one more thing.

"Thanks, Delaware One!" came Fred's grateful voice over the two way.

"No problem," I responded.

Before I left the office I called Mandy on the house phone to get a bit more detail.

"Service desk," she answered.

"Mandy, it's Harry. Where is it leaking and how bad is it?"

"This one is weird," she replied. "The resident says it's coming through the ceiling in the living room. He said it isn't like, pouring or anything, just dripping steadily from several different places near the widows."

What made this strange was that most leaks manifest themselves through the ceilings of the kitchens or bathrooms, since that's where the water supplies and drains are.

There are no kitchens near the windows in the Hancock, and only one floor plan with bathrooms near a window, but it wasn't the 08s. Of course, if undetected early, as in the case of 6905, the water will eventually spread throughout the apartment. Then it will leak through every crack in the floor slab. However, according to Mandy, the only place water was leaking into 5708 was near the living room windows.

"All right, I'll check it out."

The 08 tier in the low-rise consisted of studios, about 450 square feet, one bathroom, and a small kitchen area. The floor plan is a shotgun from the entrance to the window bay. My first stop was 5708 to see for myself exactly where the water was coming in. When the resident, a young college aged guy answered the door, I said, "I understand you have a water leak?"

"Yeah, can you come in and check it out?" he said.

I followed him toward the window bay. As I did, I could see right away that water was dripping down all along the soffit at the top of the windows. I hadn't seen anything like it before. There were no water supplies located anywhere near that area, and it wasn't raining. If it had been, it might have been a leak from a window gasket. But even so, it wouldn't have leaked as steadily or as evenly across the window as it was.

"Has it ever leaked like this before?" I queried.

"No," he replied. "I've been here a year or so and I've never

WATER, WEENIES AND WACKOS

noticed a leak before now."

"Okay, I'll check the apartment upstairs first. It's possible that the leak is coming from higher up, so it may take time to locate," I explained. "I'll let you know what happened as soon as I figure it out. Do you need some buckets or something to catch the water?"

"No. Thanks. I'll just put some rags on the window box for now."

"All right then, I'll see you later." I left to commence my expedition of discovery. I only hoped that my leak would be as easy to pinpoint as the flood the rest of the crew was dealing with in 6905. It only took them ten minutes to figure out that mess. Many times, it required hours, or even days of searching, to locate a leak.

I took the elevator to the 58th floor and walked toward the entry door for apartment 5808. I knew the guy who lived there. His name was John. He was gay -- not exactly flaming, just eccentric. He was also a player in "Shear Madness", one of the longest-running audience participation plays in the city. Nice enough guy.

He'd left complimentary tickets for me at the box office once. At that time he had just gotten the role of the gay barber. I joked with him that "it must be hard to play a barber." Truthfully, he was a pretty good actor.

I'd never been in his unit, since he had never requested service or submitted remodeling plans. I could hear nasty rap music blasting before I even got close. As I neared the door, I heard several male voices shouting, presumably to be heard above the cacophony. It sounded like a good time, which was sort of unusual given the time of day. I knocked lightly on the door and waited for a reply.

After about a minute, I knocked again, this time, a bit harder... still no answer.

Finally, I literally pounded on the door with both fists. Although the yelling had ceased momentarily, nobody came to the door. After a couple seconds, the party resumed.

Okay, I thought, I've been down this road before. They figured they could just ignore me and I would go away. Not! I'd developed a procedure for dealing with this type of situation a long time ago.

I walked down to the west service corridor, unlocked the electric meter vault, and walked in. It took a minute to locate the meter panel for 5808. Once I found it, I flipped the main breaker to the off position. That ought to get their attention! No power = no party.

I left the vault and walked back down to 5808. No more vulgar rap; lots of chatter, though. I knocked again at the door.

"Hello," answered John from the other side of the door.

"John, this is Harry, the chief engineer. I'm investigating a leak in the apartment below. I need to come in and check the plumbing."

"Um, now's not a good time. I have company."

He didn't get it. I wasn't asking. Illinois condo law provides an association with the right to emergency access to any unit within a community. Plumbing leaks in a high-rise were always considered an emergency. Of course, we rarely invoked the threat of legal action if it could be avoided.

"Yeah, I can tell," I said. "You're probably wondering why the power is out right about now, huh?"

"Um, yeah."

"Well, it's out because I just turned it off, since you wouldn't answer the door the first time I was here." Unfortunately, condo law does not provide an association the right to suspend utilities to someone's home, but, who knew?

Silence.

"Here's the deal, John. I'm not turning the power back on until you let me in to check the plumbing."

"You can't do that!" he exclaimed through the door. What he meant was that I wasn't authorized to do it. Oh well.

"I just did. If you don't let me in now, I'll notify the management office and then we can take it from there."

Again, silence.

"C'mon, John, whadaya say? Let's just work this out now and we can all stay friends, all right?"

After a few seconds and some unintelligible mumbling from within, the door was unlocked and I was allowed to enter.

"Thank you," I said as walked past John, who was trying to hide behind the door.

I noticed from the corner of my eye that he was clad only in a towel. As I headed for the front of the studio, I realized that, up until that point, I hadn't seen it all. The sight I was confronted with required complete and utter suspension of disbelief.

"You have got to be freaking kidding!" I exclaimed.

There was no carpet in the entire apartment. The floor was painted with some kind of gray epoxy. The walls were a deep shade of purple. In the middle of the room was a two foot deep, eight foot diameter inflatable kid's swimming pool with some skinny, naked Hispanic guy sitting in it, splashing water all over the place. Up near the windows was a picnic table where several men of different ages and ethnic origins, and in varying degrees of nakedness, were sitting drinking piña coladas or pink squirrels or something.

One nude-dude was standing next to a seven-foot plastic palm tree. Scattered all around the table were mirrors with what appeared to be cocaine on them. On the floor and around the fake tree were piles of beach sand. Of course, there were puddles of water everywhere, but since the floor was sealed, the only place water could leak through was where the concrete deck met the steel skeleton, up near the windows.

A fat, bald, middle-aged white guy who was sitting at the table says to me with an obvious lisp, "Hey guy, you want to party?"

"No, I don't want to party, dumbass! What the hell is wrong with you dipshits?" I shouted. I looked around at all of them. The dudes were wasted. I didn't even want to think about what they were doing before I walked in.

"Harry, we weren't bothering anyone. This is my place and it's my turn to host our club meeting," John stated from behind me. I didn't like the thought of him standing where I couldn't see him.

"How about you come over here so we can all see each other," I barked.

As John started walking over to the picnic table, a young black guy in a thong with muscles cramping his muscles and a package the size of a burrito, stood up and said, "Hey man, you can't just barge in here and start bossing us around."

He was right, to a point, of course, but there was no protocol for an incident of this nature and I didn't have the time or the desire to wait until one was developed. Besides, some of my best performances have been outright bluffs.

"Maybe not, but what I can do is leave the power off, since I now have a legitimate safety concern, with all this water all over the place. Then I can notify the management office to call the cops because you're all causing willful damage to the apartment downstairs."

Then I turned to John. "What are you guys, a bunch of retards?"

"We're just having some fun. You don't have to be so snotty. What's wrong having a little party?" he whined.

"Look, Einstein. First of all, you morons are dancing around in puddles of water with power cords lying all over the place." I pointed to the myriad of extension cords running through the pools of water to the radio and the blender as well as the little Tiki lights hanging from the soffits.

"Secondly, water is leaking down and trashing the apartment below. Even though no one thought they would have to mention specifically that you couldn't put a pool in your living room--YOU

CAN'T! And you're definitely in violation of the floor covering policy. You gotta have carpet, wood, or tile."

"C'mon guy," said fat ass.

"Shut up," I snapped. "Now look," I said as I turned back to John. "I'm not kidding. This party is over. Now!"

I turned to the dummy in the pool and said, "Get your ass out of there now." He didn't say anything, but when he stood up, I couldn't help but notice that he had an erection. "And put your meat away."

Finally I turned back to John. "I'm leaving now. In a half hour my entire crew will be here with wet vacs and a pump to empty the pool and clean up the rest of this junk. You're going to be charged for every man hour it takes to clean this mess up, including the apartment downstairs. If I were you, I'd make sure your buddies are gone and you're dressed when the guys get here."

"Fine," he said. "But you don't have to be so sassy in front of my friends."

I just glared at him and said. "I'm not in the mood, John. Fred will be bringing the camera. If you don't do exactly as I say, I'll report this entire clusterf--k to the management office as well as the resident that lives down stairs so he can file an insurance claim against you. Is that what you want?"

"No."

"Then get busy clearing this place out. My guys won't appreciate tripping over dicks while they work." Then I headed for the door.

I heard the bald guy whisper as I was leaving, "Man, that dude really sucks."

"Yeah, you wish, pillow biter!" giggled John.

On my way out, I slammed the door in a feeble attempt to quell the laughter.

꩜

The kid in 5708 bought my song and dance about a leaky dishwasher. By the time the crew finished cleaning up 5808, it was quitting time. They never got to eat their lunches that day; we didn't get the cooling coils back in service either. Although the guys were all pretty tired, they weren't too pissed off. In fact, they were kind of amused.

I had everybody up to my place for a couple of beers and some pizza and promised them all a couple of hours overtime pay to cover their missed lunch hours as well as their pain and suffering.

We laughed and drank and discussed the day's events. We also recalled previous days from hell and debated the value of higher education. In the end, we all agreed: as long as smart and sophisticated people continued to live in the Hancock, our continued employment would never be in jeopardy.

Just another Day

"Delaware Eighteen come in!" I practically screamed into the radio. I had been trying to contact our summer helper, Mike, for about fifteen minutes.

"Where the hell is that kid?" I called to Fred, who was sitting at his desk on the other side of the office.

"I don't know. The last time I saw him he was heading up to the high-rise to vacuum the floors."

Every summer, I took on a college kid or two, to cover vacation relief for the full timers. I usually just asked around and got the son of someone I owed a favor to. Most of the time, they did fine, for what we paid them. At that time, we had a young guy named Mike who was actually a school friend of the son of a friend. He'd been working with us for a couple of summers and was usually pretty reliable. The old timers liked him, mostly because they could boss him around and he wouldn't give them any lip. Everybody wanted to have their own personal flunky, and Mike fit the bill perfectly.

"Well, can you find the idiot? I've got something for him to do when he's done with the floors, I said.

Fred left the office to go find the kid and I turned to my computer. I was working on my preventive maintenance schedule and was having some difficulty with sequencing the tasks. This was why I wanted Mike. The kid was majoring in engineering and was awesome with computers.

I knew Mike could type in a couple of commands and organize everything in any order I specified. He had already figured out a way to scramble the questions on a test I'd developed for an air conditioning class I taught for the apprentices. In the midst of trying to muddle through it on my own, the phone rang.

"Engineering, Harry speaking."

"Hi, Harry. It's Mandy. I just got a call from Mr. Hershey. He said his kitchen sink exploded."

"What?! What are you talking about?" I asked skeptically. Mandy had been known to jumble information in the past.

"He said his kitchen sink exploded. He was just walking into the kitchen and suddenly, a big blast of nasty water came out of the sink drain."

"Okay. Call him back and tell him I'll come up to check it out."

I hung up the phone, saved my work on the computer, and left the office for the Hershey place. They lived in 8505, in our highest zone of apartments. The reason this was significant was that the bottom of that zone was the 82nd floor. Drain stoppages usually occurred near the bottom of the zones. I deduced that the kitchen drain line was probably clogging up and water had started to back up into their sink. When that happened, occasionally an air bubble would gurgle up through the standing water. The Hersheys were in their nineties and experience had taught me that older people tended to exaggerate when things needed attention.

After knocking at the door to 8505, I looked down the hallway to my right and noticed a tool cart outside of 8506. The guys were apparently working on something inside. After a moment, there came the sound of shuffling feet on the other side of the entry door to 8505.

"Hello," said a voice from the other side of the door.

"Good morning, Mr. Hershey. It's Harry from maintenance."

"Who?" asked the voice.

"It's Harry," I said, somewhat louder. This would be so much easier if he would just open the damn door, I thought.

"Who?"

"It's Harry from maintenance," I shouted through the door. "I'm here to check out the problem with your kitchen sink."

As the door opened he said, "Well, why didn't you say so in the first place?"

"Sorry sir," I stated flatly. "May I come in?"

"Of course -- the kitchen is this way." I didn't bother telling him that after more than ten years, I knew the floor plans of all the apartments by heart. Especially his, since I had been there at least a dozen times.

As I entered, I noticed he had black speckles all over his white shirt and his face. Then, as we turned right toward the kitchen, he stated, "I was just walking over to the sink to get some water when it just blew up."

"What exactly do you mean, 'blew up'?" I asked, as we walked into the kitchen.

"See for yourself," was all he said and pointed. "I think it happened more than once too. The kitchen was all dirty when I came in."

The entire kitchen, which was appointed with white cabinets, counters and flooring, was splattered with the same black speckle pattern that adorned Mr. Hershey's face and shirt. The pattern was definitely heavier near the sink, particularly on the underside of the cabinet directly over it.

"It scared the crap out of me when it happened," he informed me.

"I bet it did," I said as I glanced down into the sink. There wasn't any standing water, just a lot of scum and some ground up food particles. I guess it was about then that I began to have suspicions.

"Excuse me for a moment, Mr. Hershey," I said as I removed my radio from my belt.

"Delaware Five come in," I said into the radio. Delaware Five was Sergei's handle and it was his cart outside 8506.

"Delaware Five is off today, chief," came a reply. It sounded like Fred.

"Delaware Two, can you call me on the house phone at 8505 please?"

"10-4."

"Pardon me, sir." I said to Mr. Hershey. "I need to talk to Fred on your house phone."

As I was leaving the kitchen, it happened again. Pow, and there was water everywhere.

"See what I mean!" exclaimed Mr. Hershey. "It's like a geyser or something!"

Just then the house phone rang so I ran to answer it. "Fred?"

"Yeah, what's up?"

"Where's Sir Gay?"

"He had a doctor appointment or something. You approved his request."

"I did?" I queried. I couldn't keep everybody's schedules straight, which was why I needed an assistant.

"Uh...yeah."

"Well, then why's his cart outside 8506?"

"I brought Dave in to cover. He's doing simple work orders and whatever comes up, so he's using Sergei's tools," Fred replied.

"Don't tell me. He's working on a clogged kitchen sink in 8506, right?"

"Yeah, how'd you know?"

"Because I'm psychic," I replied sarcastically. "You better get up here, now." I said and hung up the phone.

Then, "Delaware Twelve come in," I shouted into the radio.

"Come back," answered Dave.

"Whatever you're doing now, stop. Stop immediately!"

"Um, okay. I mean, 10-4," he replied.

Dave was a janitor. I normally did not like having the janitors perform work orders, but when things got busy we had to spread the work out. I let Fred assign the work since he had a pretty good handle on the abilities of each guy. Personally, Dave would not have been my first choice to do anything more than mop floors. He was kind of a dipshit. I tried to run the guy through the apprenticeship program, but he couldn't handle it. He was still a nice guy though, and tried hard, so I kept him on as a janitor after he burned out of the program.

I turned to Mr. Hershey, who had just caught up with me and stated, "I'm going to have some guys come up here to clean the kitchen for you. In the mean time, I'm going to try to determine exactly what's causing this." I didn't mention that I already had a pretty good idea. "I'll be back shortly."

"All right, but will you tell me what you find out?" he asked.

"Absolutely," I replied as I walked out the door and into the hallway.

Just as the door closed, Fred got off the elevator. "Over here," I called to him as he was turning the opposite way.

He turned and asked, "So, what's up?" as he walked over to me.

"Follow me and we'll find out together." I was pretty sure I already knew exactly what was up. "Have you ever heard of the exploding sink trick?" I asked as we walked toward 8506.

"Uh…no."

"Good. Then you're about to learn something new," I said with a condescending tone.

Just as we approached the entrance to 8506, Dave was walking out.

"Hey Dave, how's it going?" I asked.

"Not too good. I've been trying to get this sink drain unclogged for over an hour," he said.

"No kidding? So what have you tried," I asked. "Did you use the rodder?"

"Nah. I've been using the Master Blaster."

"No shit?" I said as I looked sideways at Fred. "And you haven't had any luck?"

"Uh-uh. It just doesn't want to clear. The water goes down after I blast it, but when I run the taps, it just clogs up again," he stated ruefully.

The Master Blaster is a kinetic water ram. It looks like a pregnant bicycle tire pump with a pistol grip and an inverted funnel on the business end. The way it works is: you pump it up to about forty psi, push the inverted funnel down through the standing water until it is tight against the sink drain. When you pull the trigger, the compressed air slams the water, the kinetic energy is transmitted directly to the clog, and the pressure blows a hole, right through.

It is an established law of physics that liquids cannot be compressed. An automobile braking system works on a similar principle. Whatever pressure is applied to the brake pedal is duplicated at the wheel calipers, via the hydraulic lines. Unfortunately, pressure will follow the path of least resistance, which is why a braking system fails when there is a leak.

"So, did you bother to find out what's on the other side of the wall?" I asked.

"No. But what's that got to do with anything?"

"Oh, I don't know. You think maybe there's another kitchen back to back with this one? How about it, Fred? You think there's a sink on the other side of the wall?"

"Uh, yeah," was all Fred could say.

"I still don't see what that has to do with this sink being clogged," protested Dave.

"Well, why don't we all go next door and look at the result of your handiwork?" I said calmly. "And don't say anything unless I ask. Got it?"

"10-4," they replied in unison.

"So how many times did you hit it?" I asked Dave as we headed toward the entrance.

"I dunno, maybe four or five."

"Groovy."

By now it was obvious; at least to Fred and me, what had caused the "explosion" in Mr. Hershey's sink. Each time Dave blasted away at the clog in 8506, he was blowing the water right back up the sink in 8505 and all over the kitchen.

When Mr. Hershey let us in I stated, "I brought Fred and Dave here so they can survey the situation and decide what they'll need to clean up the mess, if that's all right."

"Certainly," he answered. "Hello, fellas. How's everything going?"

"Great. Thank you, sir," Fred replied. Dave just nodded.

"Well, the kitchen's down the hall," he pointed. "Harry, did you figure out the problem yet?"

"Not exactly, sir. But, I'm working on it." I still wasn't sure what I was going to tell him. I was torn between either admitting that we were a bunch of idiots or giving him some techno-crap bullshit story.

As we headed toward the kitchen, Mr. Hershey went to the living room to answer the phone. As he was walking away he said over his shoulder, "I'll be back in a minute."

When we entered the kitchen I asked, "So what do you think, guys? Ain't it awesome?!"

They both stood there slack-jawed for about a minute until Dave said, "Wow!"

"Yeah, that's what I said." Then I asked, "So Dave, you think it matters what's on the other side of a wall now?"

"Uh, I guess so, but I still don't understand how this happened," he said.

"That's because you're a dumbass!" I snapped. "This is what we call a back-to-back. Think it over. The sink you were working on is exactly opposite of this one and the clog is obviously farther down the main line."

Then, to Fred, "You know you need to plug the drain in the opposing kitchen when you use the ram, right?"

"Yeah, I guess I wasn't thinking," he replied kind of sheepishly.

"That's obvious," I said. "Maybe you and Dave can think about it while you get this mess cleaned up, huh?"

Silence.

"So what do you two think I should tell Mr. Hershey? That we're all a bunch of retards or what?"

Still; no response.

Finally, I said, "Get some more guys up here to help out, and then get that drain cleared, the right way! By the way, did you get a hold of Mike?"

"Yeah," said Fred. "He's at home and…"

"What the hell do you mean, 'he's at home?'" I cut him off.

"He says he got fired."

"What are you talking about? I haven't even seen the kid all day."

"He told me he got fired. He sounded half in the bag. I was on the phone with him when you called me on the radio, so I didn't get the rest of his story. I figured maybe you canned him and forgot about it."

Touché, Fred. That was a jab at me about not being able to remember who was working and who was off; a not so subtle reminder that I wasn't perfect either.

"Yeah, right, smartass. Just get this mess squared away. I'll deal with Mr. Hershey."

As I started toward the living room, Mr. Hershey was just hanging up the phone.

"Well, sir. We figured out what happened. It's our fault." I'd opted for honesty. "Dave was attempting to clear the kitchen drain next door and he didn't follow the correct procedure. I promise we'll have the kitchen cleaned spotless before the day is out. Please accept my apology."

"Thank you for telling me the truth, Harry. I suspected it might be something like that since there's a tool cart parked in the corridor next door. Here's the thing, though. Can you get it cleaned up before Mrs. Hershey returns from shopping? I really don't want to listen to her crying and carrying on today. And I don't think you guys do either." His raised eyebrow told me he wasn't kidding.

"We'll do our best, sir. I'll be leaving for now but Fred will be in charge. I'll be back in a while to check on their progress."

"Okey-dokey," was all he said, and I left.

※ ※ ※

"Where the hell are you?" I said into the phone. I'd finally tracked Mike down on his cell phone. Kids nowadays don't even bother with land lines.

"I'm atta home," he answered. He sounded kinda funny.

"Why are you at home? You're scheduled to work today?"

"I gotta fried (hic)," he mumbled back.

"Hey, are you drunk?" I asked because he sure sounded "fried."

"Um, uh, no. But, I sstopped at the bar in the train sst-sstashun for a couple o drinks (hic) on the way home after I got fried. I mean fired, cuz I was depreshed."

Man, the kid was shit-faced.

"What the f--k are you talking about, you got fired, dumbass? I'm your boss. I haven't even seen you today."

"Well, I was vacummuming on the ninety-firsht floor when thish really mean old lady came outta her condom, (hic), I mean condo and sstarted yelling at me about the noissse. When I tried to tell her (hic) that I was jusht doing my zhob, she told me to get the hell out the building cuz I was fried, (hic)I mean fired, and if I din't leave she was gonna call sscurity and they would (hic) kick my fat ass all the way to Mitchigan Avenue. So, I put away my shtuff and I left. And now I'm atta home"

What a putz. "Are you actually paying to go to college, doofus?" I asked.

"Well, my parensh (hic) are."

"Then you better tell them to get their money back 'cause it ain't takin'!"

"Whatcha mean, sheef?"

"Mike, are you brain dead, or what? If the old bird told you to go jump off the roof, would you do it?"

"No. I don't even have a shtupid (hic) roof key!" he blurted.

The kid's an idiot! "Well, that's one good thing," I yelled into the phone. (Sigh). "It's obvious that you're in no condition to come back to work today. But if you still want a job you better have your fat, dumb ass back here tomorrow morning, got it?"

"10-4, scheef."

"And one more thing. The next time someone fires you, check

with me first!" He tried to mumble something as I hung up the phone, but I'd already heard enough.

~~~

The door to 8505 was unlocked when I returned, so I just walked in. "Hello," I called out as I walked toward the kitchen.

As I entered the kitchen, I could see that the guys had made progress. The place was starting to look normal again; clean and unused. The Hersheys' housekeeper kept the place like a museum. Dave was standing over the sink with one hand down in it and the other on his hip. The other guys were wiping counters and detailing the appliances.

"So why are you standing there with your thumb up your ass?" I asked as I walked over.

"I'm plugging the drain so Fred can clear the sink from the other apartment with the Master Blaster," he stated.

I noticed then that he had balled up a rag over the drain and was applying pressure to it.

I was about to tell him to remove the trap and cap the drain line under the sink when Fred must have pulled the trigger because right then, a blast of filthy water came up the drain right through Dave's makeshift plug and hit us both in the face. Of course the slime rained down all over the counter and cabinets again as well.

Before I could unleash a tirade of obscenities, I noticed Mr. Hershey standing there. He looked around at all of us and the result of our latest attempt to clear the drain. Then he shook his head and shuffled out without saying a word.

Nobody said anything. As I wiped off my face with a dirty rag I reached for my radio. "Fred! Don't hit it again!" I shouted at the top of my lungs. He probably could have heard me without a radio at that point.

"Get back to work," I barked at the rest of them. "This place needs to be immaculate before the Mrs. comes home. If you're still here when she gets back, we'll all be sorry."

I left the kitchen and headed for the living room to beg for mercy from Mr. Hershey. I found him sitting cross legged on the floor with his eyes closed, his arms bent at the elbow, forearms out to the side with his fingers and thumbs pointing up. I watched him for a moment and heard him repeating something in a low voice. It sounded like;

"No-me-ar-e-um-un-gecki-oh."

"No-me-ar-e-um-un gecki-oh."

"No-me-ar-e-um-un-gecki-oh."

After a minute or so, I cleared my throat. "Um, Mr. Hershey, I'm really sorry about this screw-up. The guys will get the kitchen clean again in no time. I promise. I wouldn't blame you for being really upset."

He stopped the chanting and opened his eyes and looked at me. "Harry," he said. "I'll be ninety-three years old on my next birthday. I don't have time to get upset over little things. I want whatever time I have left to be happy and stress free. That's why I've learned to meditate. My wife, unfortunately, doesn't share my philosophy, which is why you guys need to step on it."

"Yes sir. I understand."

"Good. Now I'm going back to my happy place." Then he closed his eyes and resumed his murmuring.

I left the apartment and went next door. As I walked, I considered what Mr. Hershey had said. Maybe I needed to learn how not to sweat the small stuff.

I entered the apartment and went to the kitchen. There I found Fred standing with the Master Blaster in his hands. I reached out and gently took it from him, then laid it on the counter. "Use the rodder."

No yelling. No chastising. It wasn't easy, but I held my temper. He had surely noticed the black spots all over my shirt, which now matched Mr. Hershey's. There was no need for him to ask, or for me to explain, what had happened.

"Finish the kitchen next door first, and then clear the drain." He nodded and I left.

I returned to my office and closed the door. I sat at my desk for some time considering my universe. Why couldn't the guys, just once, all get their heads out of their butts at the same time? What was their major malfunction anyway? Was it really possible that a smart kid like Mike could be so gullible? But, the most important question of all was: how long did it take Mr. Hershey to arrive at his Nirvana?

I had no answers, but I had an idea.

Maybe the old guy was on to something. I got up, walked around to the front of my desk and sat down cross legged on the floor facing what I thought was east. I knew that the residents always faced east during the Wednesday evening yoga class. Couldn't hurt, I figured.

While I sat, I bent my arms at the elbows and put my hands out to the side with my fingers and thumbs pointing up. Then I closed my eyes and started chanting.

"No-me-ar-e-um-un-gecki-oh."

"No-me-ar-e-um-un-gecki-oh."

"No-me-ar-e-um-un-gecki-oh."

After less than a minute of reciting my incantation, I heard Fred's voice calling me over the radio. "Delaware One, come in please."

I reached for my radio in disgust. "Come back."

"Can you come back to 8505, please? Mrs. Hershey is home

and she wants to speak to you directly. Like, right now."

"10-4," I answered in defeat. What a drag. I didn't know a karma from a chi or a chi from a Zen, but, one thing I knew for sure--finding my "Happy Place," was not going to happen in my immediate future!

Epilogue

After years of serving as the resident Chief Engineer at Big John, I've come to see myself as a quarterback; when I hand off the ball, I don't expect to get it back. Usually, that's exactly the way it works. Everybody knows their jobs and they all seem to be happy doing them. Sure, there's the occasional fumble, but all in all, the team plays the game quite well.

This fortuitous circumstance has afforded me ample time to reflect, ponder, philosophize, whatever. "I am bored, therefore I think."

Unlike many people, who commit their lives to the pursuit of perfection in one specialty, I've attempted to become educated and if possible, competent in many areas. I want to do it all. I want to understand it all. I want to be a modern day Renaissance Man.

Lately, however, I've realized that I have lived here longer than any other place in my life and I have also worked here longer than at any other job. I've become lazy and spoiled; due to this arrangement. Now I'm pissed if the elevator takes more than thirty seconds to arrive. I need to quit wasting time and get busy getting busy! It's time to stop thinking and start doing again.

Let's see. I've got some dough saved up, but I'll need more. I could unload some toys; the boat, maybe even the bike, but not the flying machine. No way!

I'd get by for a while. I could probably move out to Kathy's house. Maybe start writing that book I've been thinking about, for God knows how long. Perhaps I'd even find my elusive "Happy Place." Then...

"Delaware One, come in please."

Now what? Why didn't I turn my radio off? It's already quarter to five and I'm off duty. I don't care. I'm not even going to answer. Tomorrow, I'm going down to Alan's office to hand in my radio, my keys and my two-week notice. Then, I'm outta here.

"Delaware One, come in please."

No-me-ar-e-um-un-gecki-oh. La-la-la-la-la-la. I ca-an't hear you. No-me-ar-e-um-un-gecki-oh.

Now the house phone is ringing. Crap! I know from experience that it won't stop until I answer. Next, they'll call my land line, and then it'll be the cell phone. Fine!

"What? I mean, hello," I snapped when I finally answered the house phone.

"Harry? It's Mandy. I tried you on the radio. Are you off already?"

"Yeah, whatever. What do you need?"

"I'm sorry to bother you at home, but I just got a call from the resident in 9205. Apparently, her husband is locked in the bathroom. Before you say anything, he can't unlock the door himself because he's on the floor with his hand stuck in the toilet."

"He's got his hand stuck where?"

"In the toilet."

"Why would the moron stick his hand down *there*?" Yeah, I know, I know. Where's the love?

"He was trying to get the remote control which fell into the bowl by accident."

"The remote control for what?"

"For the bidet."

EPILOGUE

I can't help it, I'm intrigued. I have to ask. "Why would anybody need a remote control to wash his own ass?"

"Because, this guy apparently has more money than brains and he ran out of things to buy. Oh, and by the way, he's naked."

Hmmm. Naked dude... on the floor...with his hand stuck in a toilet bowl. Now that's entertainment! This I've gotta see. "All right, call them back and tell them I'll be there shortly."

I gazed out over the city for a moment after I hung up the phone. To the south I could see Sears Tower and the other tall buildings in the Loop. To the west; the sunset, and the city lights running all the way out to the horizon, punctuated by the silhouette of a lone crane which appeared near to topping off yet another residential skyscraper. North; Lake Shore Drive, jammed in both directions, all the way back to Diversey, with cars stopping and going in the rush hour traffic. Man, I'm glad I don't have to deal with that.

Wait a minute. Hello, reality check! If I quit now, I'd have to get another job someplace. I mean, Kathy loves me and all that, but she wouldn't go for me lying around on my ass, smokin' weed and watching cartoons all day long. And another job would mean driving back and forth to work again. Man, would that suck. I'd have to get up at like, I don't know, five-thirty or something. Plus I'd have to pay for gas and parking. Maybe I should reconsider this whole "Renaissance Man" thing.

It's not so bad around here. Variety may be the spice of life, yada, yada, yada, but on the other hand, there's a lot to be said for comfort and security. I must be having a brain fart. Starting over now would be really hard. Hard sucks! I like easy. This job is so easy I almost feel guilty cashing my paycheck. Almost.

Only a whack-job would walk away from a gig this sweet. This place practically runs itself. In fact, if I resigned today, there would be a line of guys from the lobby to the Drive, begging to take my place by tomorrow afternoon.

Now that I think about it, a guy gets a deal like this only once in a lifetime. So all you chiefs and supers; just put away your resumes. Sorry, dudes. I'm not going anywhere. I mean, after all; at least for now...this is *MY CLOUD!*

The End

John Hancock Center

Hey, you! This is *my* cloud.

Southwest side from Harry's place.

Looking west from Harry's place

North - Bloomingdales, One Magnificent Mile, Lincoln Partk.

I wonder if it's raining down there.

Trump Tower and Willis (Sears) Tower dominate the Loop skyline.

Chicago Harbor - Filtration Plant, Navy Pier, Chicago Lock and Lake Shore Drive.

07/07/2008 10:11 pm

The west side at night.

Yeah--I'm Boomer. You wanna piece o' me? Come get some, Sally.